To Nigel
Thank you for your
inspiration – wishing you
every success

Ned

Resisting
The Soul

101 tips to free
your inspiration

A handbook for
Inspired Entrepreneurs

Nick Williams

Balloonview

Balloon View Ltd
Brenzett Place
Brenzett, Kent
TN29 0ET
www.balloonview.com

ISBN 978-1-907798-15-3

Printed in the United Kingdom for Balloon View Ltd by
CPI Bookmarque Ltd, Croydon, CR0 4TD

A CIP Catalogue record for this book is available from the British Library.

www.balloonview.com

Praise for Nick's Previous Books:

'Nick Williams offers useful and inspiring insights to explore the infinite possibilities inherent in every human being.' Deepak Chopra, author of *The Seven Spiritual Laws of Success* and *Ageless Body, Timeless Mind.*

'Nick is a great guy doing wonderful work and is an inspired teacher with much to contribute.' Dr Wayne W Dyer, author of *Manifest Your Destiny* and *Your Sacred Self.*

'Whatever you do, you can use this inspiring guide to discover purpose, meaning and passion in your work… and still pay the bills.' Paul Wilson, author of *The Little Book of Calm* and *Calm at Work.*

'Nick Williams is a wonderful man, and his book delivers a wonderful message.' Susan Jeffers, author of *Feel the Fear and Do It Anyway, End the Struggle and Dance with Life* and *Dare to Connect.*

'Nick is a visionary at work.' James Redfield, author of *The Celestine Prophecy*, and Salle Merrill Redfield, author of *The Joy of Meditating.*

'I've always believed that you should bring your heart to work. Step by step, Nick Williams shows you how.' Anita Roddick OBE, Founder, *The Body Shop International plc.*

'A book filled with wisdom but more importantly with inspiration which will lead you to use the wisdom and save your authentic life… Read and learn how to save your life, live in your heart and have magic happen. If you get the message you'll never have to do a day's work again, because it is only work if there is some place else you'd rather be.' Bernie Siegel, author of *Love, Medicine and Miracles* and *Prescriptions for Living.*

'Nick Williams has created an enormously useful way to help us discover who we are, what we want and then how to fulfil it in our work. This is a book I highly recommend.' Leslie Kenton, author of *Journey to Freedom.*

'I firmly believe that we all came with a unique purpose, but finding that purpose can take a lifetime, unless of course you read this inspiring and magical book to hasten the process.' Hazel Courtney, award-winning health writer.

'…a joy to read. It sparkles with inspiration and delight, and is packed with ideas that will help you discover your life's work – and create a life you truly love. Whether you hide under the bedclothes on Monday mornings, or just feel bored or dissatisfied at work, you need this book!' Gill Edwards, author of *Living Magically and Stepping into the Magic*.

'Nick not only goes about placing our work into its true perspective in our lives but he also provides the criteria for what has meaning and value in life – happiness and fulfilment! This is an excellent and well written book on meaningful work. Nick does all the work for us in setting profound and everyday truths down in an easy and palatable form.' Dr Chuck Spezzano, author of *If It Hurts, It Isn't Love* and *Happiness is the Best Revenge*.

This book overflows with the richest wisdom of the heart and positive skills for self-appreciation, open-hearted living and success. Nick Williams gets to the core of the power to make our lives what we would have them be. Read this magnificent work, enjoy, grow and soar!' Alan Cohen, author of *The Dragon Doesn't Live Here Anymore, Joy is My Compass and Handle with Prayer*.

'This inspiring book provides the map and compass that will guide you to that sought-after destination of being able to fulfil your true potential, through your natural vocation. Use it!' Colin Turner, corporate speaker and author of *The Eureka Principle* and *Swimming with the Piranhas Makes You Hungry*.

'Beautiful sequencing of proven principles – bursting with passion and wisdom.' Dr Stephen Covey, author of *The Seven Habits of Highly Effective People*.

Acknowledgements

Thanks as ever to Helen Bee for our fifteen years of love, encouragement and friendship. To my Mum, Pam, for her continued love and support, and to the memory of my father, Harold, and his enduring love.

To Niki Hignett for friendship, his brilliance and our constant re-invention, and Ali for continuing to generously loaning him to our business.

To Steven Pressfield for inspiring me. He has helped me understand resistance and inspired me to overcome my own.

To Sue Cheshire and her husband Kent Allen for welcoming us to Green Oak Barn, and all at the Global Leaders Academy and especially Michael Van Clarke for inspiration.

To Adam Stern, Matt Ingrams and Martin Wenner for eighteen years of friendship – and counting. And to my brothers in MKP and the Elders Group.

To Ed Peppitt – you continue to be a real find!

Thanks Caroline Swain for editing this book

All our friends at the Pia Bella in Kyrenia and to John and Elaine in Bellapais.

Chris and Sylvina for friendship, and to Howard and Trish for friendship.

Rick and Helen for continuing precious friendship.

To Dr Robert Holden, as ever, for generosity and friendship and being a travelling companion, and for helping with this book title. Thanks also to his wife Hollie for friendship and love.

To Charlie Jordan for your friendship and unending conversation.

To 'The Group' – Juliette, Peter, Jan and Linda and the memory of Catherine.

To Jeff Allen – soul brother whose love and insight always save my ass when I hit rock bottom, and for being a good friend. To his wife Sue and to Julie Wookey. and to Chuck and Lency Spezzano for continuing inspiration.

Thank you Polly MacDonald for your support and coaching. Thank you Peter for continuing games of pool at the Eight Club. Thanks to Judy Piatkus for friendship, encouragement and connections. Thanks to Art Giser for your simple and powerful Energetic NLP work.

And always to *A Course in Miracles*, for being the beacon of light on my way home.

To all our presenters at Inspired Entrepreneur for sharing so generously and for all the tribe – the people who come to our events and share themselves in the world.

Thanks to Susie Lomax, Angela Taylor, Jo West, Chris Pritchard and Wendy Hannon for supporting our events and meeting and greeting and taking care of people so wonderfully.

Contents

1. You are an instrument, here to bring into
   existence new life and creations.
2. Resistance is largely unconscious.
3. Remember that something wonderful came
   before your resistance.
4. Learn the difference between resistance,
   necessity and intuition.
5. Resistance can actually be a pointer,
   and a North Star.
6. Not showing up is actually an act of arrogance.
7. Dare to go deeper to understand that all
   resistance is a conspiracy against your
   goodness, greatness and brilliance.
8. Recognise that the work you are most likely
   to resist is the work you were put on this
   planet to do.
9. You are here to do something beautiful.
10. You have a specific personal purpose
    and a destiny.
11. You are custodian of projects and gifts.
12. You can't take all the credit for your brilliance.
13. Do believe in Heaven.

14. Become a servant of the great mystery.
15. Recognise the real purpose of resistance.
16. Have long-term goals.
17. Become the initiating force in your life.
18. Own your fear so it doesn't own you.
19. Step out of your own shadows and into the centre stage.
20. Recognise that you might be in recovery.

21. Recognise that there are times when your great intelligence can also be an impediment.
22. Recognise and relinquish your need to be special.
23. Over-planning is procrastination in disguise.
24. Resist the temptation to "just need to know a little bit more" before you start.
25. Recognise that resistance can be really nasty.
26. Don't use your problems and your suffering to define you.
27. Recognise the difference between an obstacle and an excuse.
28. Give up your worry that you'll be copied.
29. Don't leach on the greatness of others – find the greatness in you.
30. Other people often serve as the mouthpieces of your unconscious resistance.
31. Forgive yourself your own self-defeating behaviour.
32. Understand your grandeur and your grandiosity.
33. Resistance thrives on competition and comparison.
34. Decide when to call off the search.
35. Recognise fights and power struggles as resistance.
36. Resistance can be building other people's dreams and not investing in your own.
37. Resistance is the cause of pain, not a protection against pain.

38. Be vigilant to your Master Fear.
39. Beware of busy-ness and over-enthusiasm.
40. You can live up to your principles to your imperfect best.
41. Stop looking for short-cuts, and invest your energy into your work.

42. Turn pro.
43. The pro acts now and invests in anticipation of success.
44. Quit waiting to be discovered and reveal yourself instead.
45. Quarantine your drama.
46. Remember that relinquishing resistance can be a long-term process.
47. Be scared regularly.
48. Recognise the difference between the suffering ethic and birth pains.
49. Master your ego.
50. Work for love first – and be very willing to be paid.
51. Sometimes, act in faith and in anticipation of inspiration.
52. Recognise it's all fear.
53. Trust your own uniqueness and don't try to copy others.
54. Be willing to invest your energy in projects with unknown outcomes.
55. When delaying tactics are no longer working, resistance goes for your jugular.
56. You do need to feel safe but not in the way resistance tells you.
57. Don't invest too much of your identity in what you do.
58. Demystify inspiration.
59. Sometimes resistance just wants to take you out.
60. As a pro, you like to keep things simple.

61. Choose to be of service to life.
62. Start before you feel ready.
63. Learn to feed your inspiration and starve your resistance.
64. Give yourself permission to make mistakes and to learn and still be OK.
65. Embrace your fear of people being jealous of you.
66. Give yourself fully and hold nothing back.
67. Bust the myth that successful people obviously don't have resistance.
68. Exercise your creative muscles every way you can.
69. Be willing to die and be reborn.
70. It is usually not about the money.
71. Show up for your part of the deal.
72. Understand it is baby steps all the way.
73. You learn the "how to" do it as you go.
74. Even when resistance feels awful, you can move through it.
75. Now is always a good time.
76. Break your isolation.
77. Don't try to solve problems you don't have yet.
78. Get a few failures under your belt.
79. Don't resist the rehearsals, they lead you to mastery.
80. Support your success by creating a supportive structure.
81. Learn to self-validate.
82. Throw your heart over the fence and make a commitment.

My own story around resistance

For most of my life I was in resistance and didn't even realise it. I thought I was being sensible, playing safe, trying to be how I thought others wanted me to be. For the first half of my life, I thought it was normal to be hard on myself, to squash most of the good ideas, to judge myself as a being a silly dreamer and so much of my energy went into trying to dull the sense of loneliness, and at times the meaninglessness, I experienced. I felt inadequate and stayed in work I didn't really enjoy for longer than was probably necessary. My own resistance led me to live a smaller life, to drink to excess, undermine and sabotage myself, be unkind to myself and those around me. It even led me to suicidal tendencies. I was pretty unhappy. I did know joy, happiness and love too, but nowhere near the extent I do today.

Much of my pain was, I always sensed there was someone in my heart I could become, but then I dismissed this as me deluding myself in fantasy. I felt imprisoned by my own fears, thoughts and emotional patterns. But the word resistance didn't even figure in my vocabulary. All I knew was that I was slow to do what I knew in my heart I wanted to be doing. Eventually, I did find the courage to quit my corporate career and start my own business as a promoter, coach and speaker.

Even when I got deeply involved in the worlds of personal growth and human potential, part of me judged myself harshly for needing all this inspiration malarkey. I wondered why I couldn't just be content with a material existence. I was still tempted to try to distort myself into a version of myself that I thought would be OK, loveable and acceptable.

In 2004, I was recommended to read the book, *The War of Art* by Steven Pressfield. As I read his book, suddenly my whole life made more sense. I had simply been in resistance and Steven had simply articulated what resistance was and how it operated in a way that I had never fully understood until then. I wasn't mad, I was in resistance, and now I knew it. I was liberated to begin to understand that I was conspiring against my best self and the level of my resistance was in direct proportion to the passion I had, and the ultimate success I could create.

And now I have become more of that person I sensed in my heart I could become. I realise I have a self to become, a calling to enact and projects to bring into existence. I can't be anyone I want, I need to keep listening to my soul and bring the essence of me into greater existence. It's been a baby step by baby step process of facing fear after doubt after uncertainty. But I have consciously chosen it and it has initiated an ongoing journey of transformation. I know it is possible to get beyond resistance and give birth to your greatest self. And it's daily work.

So do I still experience resistance? Yes, I do. But I joke and say, "Now I resist with awareness!" I know what I am doing, and I still do it, but I don't do it for so long. There is always a stronger part of me now that wants to push through it. And sometimes resistance comes in a new form that I don't quite recognise and get a handle on immediately. I know I will experience resistance for the rest of my life, that it is a daily battle. But I also now know I can beat it, and bring forth new life, ideas and projects through me into the world. That excites me.

And what is my one piece of advice to you that's worked for me? Listen to my heart and then show up, and show up *before* you feel ready. Excessive preparation is just another form of resistance.

Why I am so passionate about overcoming resistance and freeing our unlived potential

I believe that within each of us two lives exist. The life we live, and the life of potential, the unlived life within us. What stands between the two is resistance. I would go as far as to say that resistance is the most toxic force on the planet and stops us being who we are and were born to be. Each of us has a brilliance, access to a God given genius, and resistance's declared goal is to stop you shining your own particular and unique light. As powerful as your own call to evolve and self-realise is, the forces of resistance are arrayed against you.

I have come to truly believe that unfulfilled potential is one of the greatest problems on the planet. If all the love, talent, gifts and abilities, that currently lie dormant within the billions of human beings on the planet, were unleashed, the world would be transformed. All these gifts and talents already exist *in potential* and whilst problems with the economy, education and inequality play a part in squashing our potential, the greatest obstacle of all, is our resistance. And the saddest part of it is, that most people don't understand their resistance. They may simply believe there is nothing more within them, or they know there is more within them, but are at a loss to know what stops them letting it out.

When I was young, I had a vision of who I might become, but struggled to access and release that person and wondered if I might be deluding myself. I didn't know resistance then, so my own unfulfilled potential drew me towards unhappiness, depression, negativity, loneliness, addictions, judgment and criticism of others, envy and other self-defeating and self-destructive behaviours. I thought that was just life.

I honestly believe that if everyone were able to realise their own gifts and potential, the pharmaceutical companies would be in big trouble. The suppliers of alcohol would be in big trouble too. I think there would be fewer wars and more co-operation. Why? Because people would be happy and fulfilled and they wouldn't need to try to blot out their pain. Happy people want others to be happy too. Inspired people want to inspire others, not control and manipulate them. The natural tendency of people who have realised their own potential is to generously encourage and support others to do the same. Potential requires you to open your heart and mind and confront your own demons. Eventually you realise that all the significant demons are within and ultimately you are only ever fighting yourself. Once you have illuminated your own darkness, you see the darkness in the world as a call for your love and leadership.

I believe you know that there is a voice in your heart that is telling you, as it has ten thousand times, that the calling and the gifts are yours and yours alone. You know it, and no-one needs to tell you. Reading this book will help you take a step to trusting your heart and releasing your calling.

The Five Keys:

Key 1   The nature of resistance and the purpose it seeks to serve

Key 2   The nitty gritty of resistance and how it shows up – need to recognise it – know the enemy

Key 3   Turning pro – the attitude of a spiritual and creative warrior

Key 4   The professional's tool kit - strategies to get beyond resistance

Key 5   Your higher power and skilfulness – serving your brothers and sisters

Key 1:

The nature of resistance and the purpose it seeks to serve

I do believe that each of us is here now in life for a purpose. That feeling of "I was put on earth to do something magnificent" is true. What you do matters. Who you are matters. I believe that each of us has a brilliance, something that came with our creation. We promised to bring that gift into the world now, so that *we* could be happy and fulfilled and also help to transform our little corner of creation at the same time. There is a world waiting to be born through you. You have a higher purpose for being here now and your playing small doesn't serve the world. We don't need any more martyrs – we need empowered, creative people who are committed to a great life for themselves and everyone else. We need people who are leaders in their own lives, who, as they show up as their best selves, inspire others to do the same.

And this is precisely what resistance doesn't want. It wants you to remain self-conscious, self-absorbed, afraid and playing small and living a pinched life, if not materially, then spiritually and creatively. Resistance is the enemy of your higher purpose – it wants you to stay asleep and forget, focused on your own lower nature – material survival and gratification. Your fears unseen and unfaced, become your limits without you even realising it. It wants to keep you asleep to your higher purpose and the happiness and deep fulfilment that would go along with that. Resistance is all the ways that you are not encouraging and supporting your own growth, happiness and success.

Most of our fears are not conscious to us. We don't even know most of them are there. They are deeply hidden and because they seem invisible, it can be hard for you to realise that you are in a battle with a hidden enemy. But you know its effects – it's a repelling force, it wants to create distance between you and your work here. It wants to scare and delay you, distract you, and distort your thinking. It is insidious – it lies, cheats, bullies, scares and manipulates you into being less than you are. Resistance is not a battle that you ever win forever. Each day is a new round in the ring.

Resistance aims itself at your very genius and brilliance – it is the shadow cast by the light that is within you. It wants to stop you showing up with your priceless brilliance, with the gifts and talents that you'd most love to share with your fellow human family. Resistance would rather play god and stop you, than allow your divine qualities to flow.

Nothing immunises you from resistance – it brings you face to face with your shared humanity. I have coached millionaires, leaders, happy people, people who are dying, broke people, unemployed people, creative and uncreative people. When it comes to showing up authentically in the world, it's a level playing field. We are all gift bearers, we all have potential, we all have demons, fears and vulnerabilities.

I obviously can't prove I am right, but in my heart I believe that all the answers to the problems that we face in the world already exist within the people here. The talents, potential and gifts that go *unexpressed* within most human beings are massive. I can speak personally – all that I am doing today – the books, the programmes, the inspiration and love – were in me in potential twenty years ago and now they are out in the world. I don't believe I am at all special. I think the same untapped potential exists within most people, if not everyone. I have just listened to my own inner impulses and inspiration and kept showing up.

1. You are an instrument, here to bring into existence new life and creations.

"The art of life is to live in the present moment, and to make that moment as perfect as we can by the realization that we are the instruments and expression of God Himself."

Emmet Fox,
Spiritual Author and Lecturer 1886-1951.

Your job is as an agent of the infinite, here to bring into existence within the realms of time and space, new life, creations, gifts and talents, that wouldn't exist in this world without you. You are here to be an alchemist, to create something out of the seeming nothingness of a thought and an idea. Serving this higher purpose is what will make your life meaningful. You are not the originator of your ideas, they come from another sphere of existence, from the realm of possibility where all ideas exist as thoughts but not yet as physical manifestations. When you are most inspired, you are alert to the ideas that would most thrill you to bring into existence. Your resistance will have you believing that the purpose of your existence is purely material – to make money, be safe, and do what you need to do to survive. Recognise the distinction between what can be done *by* you and what can be done *through* you. Whilst the source of your creations is another realm, it needs you to make them real in this plane of existence. You are necessary, they wouldn't happen without you. You are a pipeline to the divine, and resistance is simply the kinks in your pipeline!

Freedom project: Ask yourself, "What wants to come into existence through me?" – you are a conduit, a midwife, not an originator. Tune into what the higher intelligence is inviting you into. How is greater intelligence whispering to you? What is your next assignment? What are you pregnant with? What is inspiration nudging you into next? Listen and be receptive, and capture the answers that come to you. Have the courage to stop being so busy and give yourself time and space and safety from the voices that keep saying "Keep busy or nothing will happen and it will all fall apart". Put yourself in the presence of the influences that nourish your creativity, so that new life can emerge from you.

2. Resistance is largely unconscious.

"The goal of therapy is to make the unconscious conscious."

Sigmund Freud,
Founder of Psycho-analysis.

You may not recognise that you are in resistance. It may not even be *your* resistance. It may be your early upbringing programming you with others' thoughts and fears. You may not have had the language or insight before reading this book to recognise what your resistance is. You may only know yourself as restless, unfulfilled, bored, cross with yourself. You may have told yourself that you have simply been sensible and responsible. You may not have realised that this is a sign that your calling is calling, but your resistance is doing all it can to keep you asleep. So, as you become more aware of your resistance, don't use it as another way of beating yourself up. Use it as information. Utilise the opportunity for self-compassion, as you recognise the patterns that tried to stay hidden so they could run you. Celebrate your awareness and know that this will then open up greater choice and freedom in your life.

Freedom project: Understand and accept that you do have resistance, even if you hadn't realised it clearly until now. This is an important step in your wakening and liberation.

3. Remember that something wonderful came before your resistance.

"Resistance arises second. What comes first is the idea, the passion, the work we are so excited to create that it scares the shit out of us."

Steven Pressfield,
Author of War of Art

Resistance is not a primary force but a response and a reaction. Your inner critic only emerges *because* you are doing or about to do something significant and creative. The volume of your resistance is usually proportionate to your proximity to your creative brilliance. Your problem is not that you have an inner critic – we all have one – your challenge is how you relate to it and get beyond it. Some impulse came before the resistance, triggered it, awoke the slumbering dragon. That impulse came from a deeper and truer place within you, the grandeur within you, the highest self that you are. Resistance is simply your mind's fearful response to your heart and soul's inspiration.

Freedom project: You are not your resistance. It is a part of your make up. Regularly listen to and acknowledge that there is a part of you that is bigger and more powerful than your resistance.

4. Learn the difference between resistance, necessity and intuition.

"Every time I've done something that doesn't feel right, it's ended up not being right."

Mario Cuomo,
Lawyer and Former Governor of New York

Sometimes it's not resistance – you just don't want to do something and it's OK not to want to do it. If you are trying to push yourself to do something that goes against your grain or doesn't light up your heart, it will be tough. Yet often we are taught to do exactly that. Don't try to override your heart with logic. I spent much of my life overriding natural instincts, to do what I thought I should. Of course, there are duties and responsibilities that we all have to acknowledge. But you also need those places of joy and deep personal alignment with your inner self. There are gifts, talents and ideas inside you, that long to emerge and be known in this world. Stop searching for happiness and follow your joy. Your best work will always come from expressing yourself rather than going against yourself. How do you tell the difference between resistance and your intuition telling you that something isn't right? If you have never felt inspired and excited then it may not be resistance. If you got inspired and then lost that inspiration, resistance probably crept in.

Freedom project: Make a list of all the things you know you really don't want to do, and a list of things you know you'd love to do and are resisting. Start working through your list of resistances and try to delegate some of what you don't want to do.

5. Resistance can actually be a pointer, and a North Star.

"Whichever way the wind of resistance is coming from, that's the way to head – directly into the resistance. And the closer you get to achieving the breakthrough your genius has in mind, the stronger the wind will blow and the harder the resistance will fight to stop you."
Seth Godin in Linchpin

If you didn't care, if there wasn't love, passion, inspiration and devotion, there would simply be indifference. The fact *that* you resist means there is something *to* resist. And it is that precious impulse that we talked about at the beginning. Your ego will tell you that it is protecting you from career and social suicide, looking stupid, failing, going broke or mad, but actually it is lying to you so that you will stay in fear and not show up fully in your life. It wants you to remain ruled by fear rather than be liberated to your full potential. Recognise that resistance is repressed energy. It is the level of fear and blockedness you have. The amount of your resistance directly correlates to the amount of creative energy and talent you will have, as you unblock yourself. Or as some people express it, "The bigger your purpose, the bigger your problems."

Freedom project: Keep a list of the things that you get most scared about, what you keep talking yourself out of and the wonderful ideas you have that won't go away. You have your North Star.

6. Not showing up is actually an act of arrogance.

"Success means we go to bed at night knowing that our talents and our abilities were used in a way that served others. We're compensated by grateful looks in people's eyes, whatever material abundance supports us in performing joyfully at high energy, and the magnificent feeling that we did our bit today to serve the world.... Sharing our gifts is what makes us happy.... God does not demand sacrifice."

Marianne Williamson in *A Return To Love*.

You've been created by Life for a mighty purpose and you playing smaller and being less than you are capable of being, doesn't serve you or the world. When you invest energy in creating stories as to why you aren't ready and aren't good enough, you are fighting with creation. You have very little understanding of how your gifts and talents may be utilised in this world. But a greater intelligence has. Out of the books I have written, talks and workshops I have offered, events I have organised and broadcasts I have made, I would reckon that I am probably aware of 1 or 2% of the impact I have made. And in a way, it is not my business to know or want to know the impact I have had. I am an agent of the Infinite carrying out divine impulses, willingly. This doesn't mean being a martyr, quite the opposite. You are here to do what you love and what makes your heart sing. *And never do it for the money.* Don't go to work to make money, go to work to spread joy. Put aside, "Yes, but I could never get paid to do that." How on earth do you know? It's such a self-betraying thing to say. You can never see the end result from the start line. You have to be in the game to see how it's really played. You often can't figure out how something is going to turn into income at the beginning, but it can do.

Freedom project: Get beyond the self judgement and criticism and commit to showing up in the world to the best of your abilities. Remind yourself, "I am a unique expression of Life."

7. Dare to go deeper to understand that all resistance is a conspiracy against your goodness, greatness and brilliance.

"All resistance is a conspiracy against ourselves"
**Jeff Allen, Psychology of Vision Master Trainer
and co-author of *How Love Works***

In essence that is what resistance is about – it is the way your ego conspires against the power and brilliance of your spirit. All resistance is actually a form of self-attack and self diminishment. Resistance is also a form of control – usually self-control because we are afraid of surrendering and being in the flow. Then your heart would be in charge, not your ego. So be willing to start moving in the direction of your fear – most of us are brought up to move away from our fears and avoid them. As a creative soul, you recognise that the greatest juice of your life comes from moving in the direction of your fear and seeing what talent lies within and just beyond your fear. In your heart, as a creative soul you know that each time you face the things that scare you, several things happen: there is usually a gift; you grow in confidence; you liberate yourself and feel a little freer. As a creative soul, as a leader, you are paid to be scared, regularly. If you are not at the edge of your comfort zone, you are probably not growing.

Freedom project: Remind yourself of the goodness, creativity and power at the heart of you. It is still there, waiting to be remembered and re-discovered.

8. Recognise that the work you are most likely to resist is the work you were put on this planet to do.

"Is it that rational and logical that anybody should feel afraid of what they were put on this earth to do? And what is it about creative ventures that make us worry for each other's mental health?"

**Elizabeth Gilbert,
Author of Eat Pray Love**

It's strange but true that in my 20 years of personal and professional experience, the closer you get to your life's work, your spiritual purpose, the work you were born to do, the more likely resistance is to kick in. Unless it is your spiritual destiny to be a telemarketer or work on a supermarket check-out (which it could be), you are likely to experience resistance. When you do a job in an organisation, resistance doesn't surface that much. Reluctance yes, but not resistance. But if you want to write the book that has been incubating in your heart for years, quit your high paid but unfulfilling corporate job, start the enterprise that you have been planning every day and on every holiday, or start that blog to share your intimate thoughts to inspire and support your fellow human beings, *then* you will likely, but not inevitably, experience resistance.

Freedom project: Recognise the bigger the fear, the bigger the gift. The thing you most resist could well be your purpose, the thing that will most fulfil you as you start doing it.

9. You are here to do something beautiful.

"Your holiness blesses the world"

A Course in Miracles

I don't believe that you are here randomly, just by some combination of molecules and reactions. You are more than biological, you are an emotional and spiritual being. I believe you have made a promise to be here, now. You were born carrying a promise to make this world better in some way, and there is a yearning in you to make good on that promise, and you can't suppress that yearning forever. You are being inspired to awaken, as millions of others are, and the goal of resistance is to stop you and keep you asleep.

Freedom project: Honour the preciousness of your creation. Spend time with others who are awake or awakening and who make you feel good about yourself.

10. You have a specific personal purpose and a destiny.

"You are your own patron, benefactor, wise aunt. You are the one who must plan your great adventures-and make your great escapes."

Eric Maisel,
Author and Advocate of creativity

And part of you, the deepest part of you, knows what that is, in direction if not in detail. You need to get honest with yourself. One form of resistance is prolific self-delusion and self-denial. You try to pretend that you don't know what in your heart you do know. It's very tempting to buy into the idea that you can be anything you want to be. You just have to decide who you want to be and you can set out to become it. But I think there are deeper dynamics at work. I think you are an eternal soul, the veteran of many lifetimes. And you have set up a curriculum for this lifetime. You have a person to become, a calling to enact, obstacles to overcome, gifts to share. So your job is to look deep inside yourself and look for the promise you made, the seeds of who you truly are already, that you promised to become. Yes, now you feel scared about the promise you made. Now you are here, it can seem impossible. But you are not alone. You can do it. And I believe that everyone already knows what that purpose is. You can deny it to yourself, you can forget it, but some part of you knows very clearly why you are here.

Freedom project: Don't try to live someone else's life, it won't make you happy. So what is your soul's promise? Who have you promised to become? How bright did you promise to shine in this life? What would inspire you? Where are you hiding out? Ask your heart, "Who did I promise to be in this life and What did I promise to do?"

11. You are custodian of projects and gifts.

"Among us, there are people who can turn old plastics into jewellery, teach children to cook, inspire an MP, design sustainable homes, chair community meetings, give healing massages, forage for wild food, create powerful film documentaries, write songs and make clothes. When we hold back our contribution, our community suffers. We deprive our community, just as we deprive ourselves of the pleasure of offering our gift."
Corinna Gordon Barnes, Coach

You are here to bring love, gifts, creativity, beauty and transformation into existence in this world. They won't exist until you show up. It can sound grandiose, but is literally true. You promised to do this. Will you make good on your promise? Think about the many people who have touched your life, inspired, encouraged and supported you. What if they hadn't shown up? Might you have given up? Might your life be poorer? Of course, it would. In the same way, you hold the key to other people's success, inspiration and hope. The world needs what you've got inside you. Heaven has full confidence in your creative gifts and your ability – trust heaven not your ego.

Freedom project: Ask yourself what were you made for and what gifts and activities give you most joy.

12. You can't take all the credit for your brilliance.

"There is a Light in you which cannot die, Whose Presence is so holy that the world is sanctified because of you... The Light in you is what the Universe longs to behold."

A Course in Miracles

But you can take the credit for showing up with it – your brilliance came with your creation. It was put within you by God, the Universe, Heaven or whatever you believe in, or if you don't believe in a higher power, then it comes from the highest in your humanity. And you can take the credit for beating your resistance and showing up and sharing that brilliance. With God as the source of all creation, your job is simply to express that bit of creation that you are inspired to give form to.

Freedom project: What do you most want to show up with in this world?

13. Do believe in Heaven.

"Heaven is chosen consciously"

A Course in Miracles

Sometimes, we get through resistance by some kind of surrender. There are times when we pray and ask for help. My friend Dr. Chuck Spezzano suggests: "Put it in Heaven's hands." But often that seems not to work. Then there are the times when unseen hands do seem to work within us and we realise that *Amazing Grace* is not just a song title, but a reality. Some deep resistance can only be overcome by surrendering to something greater, we cannot consciously do it. It is not just done by you, but through you too, your part in that is a willingness. From your limited perspective, you can't see how all the bits of the jigsaw fit together. You have no idea how your gifts could best be used. Heaven has a marketing plan for you. It knows what you can become and what gifts you uniquely have and the impact that your love does have and could have. Heaven wants to utilise you for transforming some corner of creation that would fully excite and thrill you. God is complete and unconditional love, and nothing else. It's that simple. There is no anger, jealousy or judgement in God. Everything else is misunderstanding and human creation that we project onto God.

Freedom project: Trust, trust, trust.

14. Become a servant of the great mystery.

"In reality, we are servants of the Mystery. We were put here on earth to act as agents of the Infinite, to bring into existence that which is not yet, but which will be, through us."

**Steven Pressfield,
Author of War of Art**

You don't have to know where your ideas come from – just act on them! You don't even need to know what impact you will have. That's not really your business. Inspiration is ultimately a mystery. One lesson in *A Course in Miracles* says that "Your part is essential in God's plan for salvation." You don't know how your gifts can be used. You don't need to know how electricity works to turn on the light, or how the internal combustion engine works to drive to the shops, but you know that they do work. Inspiration exists and it works for you whatever its glorious and mysterious source, forever offering you your next assignments and brilliant projects. Your job is to bring those ideas into this earthly realm, to give them your hands, feet and expression. Your job is to faithfully execute, to become skilful and to add your unique expression to them. Just be glad that the technology of ideas and inspiration exists and be their faithful servant. Become a servant of the great Mystery.

Freedom project: Connect with your higher purpose regularly. What do you love bringing into this world?

15. Recognise the real purpose of resistance.

"Before the dragon of Resistance reared its ugly head and breathed fire into our faces, there existed within us a force so potent and so life-affirming that it made Resistance freak out and load up the sulphur and brimstone."

Steven Pressfield,
Author of War of Art

It claims to be your friend. Resistance whispers in your ear that it is saving you from pain, failure, looking stupid, being rejected, going broke, wasting your life on fruitless ventures. On a bad day, you do actually believe that. But in your heart, you know that resistance is actually keeping you from your juice and from the magnificence of your life. It is deceiving you into believing that you are a purely physical being rather than an amazing spirit in a body. It is keeping you from your talent and power. It is trying to keep you afraid and asleep. It's got some pretty convincing arguments, but none of them is true.

Freedom project: Remember - whatever resistance may whisper in your ear, it is not your friend. It does not have your best interests at heart. Listen to another voice.

16. Have long-term goals.

"It is very important to generate a good attitude, a good heart, as much as possible. From this, happiness in both the short term and the long term for both yourself and others will come."

The Dalai Lama, Spiritual Leader

I have been continually inspired by one of our alumni with whom I have worked over a number of years. Cali Bird shared with me eleven years ago that she had many dreams and long-term goals. Two specific ones were: to have a book published, and to share a speaking stage with me. In January 2011, she published her first book entitled *Don't Give Up Your Day Job* and on 12th April 2011 we presented an evening talk together for the Inspired Entrepreneur London audience. As she shared some of her experiences that evening, she talked about how that talk was the fulfilment of those two of her long term goals. In truth, you never know whether the time, love and energy you invest in projects are going to create the success that in your mind you want them to create. Although this is the seventh book I have written, there are probably twenty books that I have started and not finished over the years. You need to invest creatively to learn and grow. You may write three books that don't get published in order to develop the skill and flair that will get the fourth published and touch a nerve with people. Investing energy in projects is an act of faith. But I don't think it is ever wasted. Whatever the outcomes, you will learn something, even if it is "How to make every mistake under the sun." Making all those mistakes may then open the doorway to success for you. There will always be a gift and a blessing, when you are willing to see it.

Freedom project: Have a long term vision of who you want to become and what you want to contribute. That vision will pull you forward through the challenging times.

17. Become the initiating force in your life.

*"Initiative is that exceedingly rare quality that impels a
person to do that which ought to be done, without being
told to do it."*

Napoleon Hill, author of *Think and Grow Rich*

As you break through your resistance, you become an
initiator, and as you become an initiator, you will need to
break through your resistance. Initiation can be a scarce
resource. So many of us have been taught for much of
our life to respond to instructions, to wait to be given
permission to do something and to be compliant. Or
we may have become rebellious and done the opposite
of what we thought we were expected to do. As a truly
creative soul, you are neither compliant nor rebellious –
you act from a deeper sense of truth and inspiration that
originates in your true self, your soul. So commission
and lead yourself – as an artist, you follow your Muse,
your sense of inspiration. You are following your inner
voice. There are probably very few factors outside of
you putting pressure on you to start your enterprise,
write your book, pick up your spiritual practice or create
your CD set. Indeed, many of the voices outside you are
probably questioning you or may be actively telling to not
to do it. You need to become CEO of yourself, your own
commissioning editor, your own advocate. It helps to sit
down with yourself and have a meeting and look at your
projects and decide which ones you are going to do, and
then become accountable to yourself for their delivery.

Freedom project: What are you waiting to start? What can
you start – even in tiny ways – today, now? Say yes to starting
to express what wants to come into existence through you.

18. Own your fear so it doesn't own you.

"People ask me to teach them how they can be fearless, and I answer by telling them that I can't teach them that, but I can teach them how to have fear and do their creative work anyway."

Julia Cameron,
Author of the Artists Way

When you are afraid of your fears and keep them at a distance, they have a power over you. They have you. You live your life constrained by them, denying them, trying to control them or defending against them. When you can maturely own and name your fears, they begin to lose their power. Fear breeds by staying hidden and unnamed. Owned and named, fear is less powerful. When you can say clearly to yourself, "I am afraid of being shamed or humiliated, I am afraid of going broke, I am afraid I won't finish this project, I am afraid no-one will buy my book or I am afraid that I won't find clients for my business," then you take back your power. That is the key: feel the fear and do it anyway. Resistance loves it when you wait for your fear to subside because it knows that there is unlikely to be a fear free day. But resistance hates it when you act in the face of your fear, because it knows it has lost some control over you. Resistance hates courage.

Freedom project: Write a list of your fears, all of them. Own them without feeling bad. "I am afraid of...." And then choose to act anyway.

19. Step out of your own shadows and into the centre stage.

"Shadow artists often choose shadow careers – those close to the desired art, even parallel to it, but not the art itself."
Julia Cameron in The Artists Way

One form of resistance is to be close to what you'd love to do, but not quite doing it. You are in the vicinity of it, but standing in the shadows. My own example was when I was involved in running one of the world's premier mind body spirit lecture series in London, called Alternatives. I loved it for many years, and then became a little bored. "How could this be?" I thought. I had dreamed of being immersed in the world of personal development and spiritual growth. I was organising talks for many of the world's leading voices, such as Dr Wayne Dyer, Dr Deepak Chopra, Susan Jeffers, John Gray, Byron Katie and Eckhart Tolle. Then it dawned on me, "I don't want to be the one organising the talks anymore, I want to be the one giving the talks!" it was a moment of inspiration and realisation followed by massive resistance. "Who would want to listen to me? What have I got to say?" etc etc. But it led me to step up my fledgling speaking career, to have the courage to pursue my own talent and write my first book. Then the world began to open up for me. But it took enormous courage for me to recognise that I was living a shadow life and then to confront my own resistance to truly showing up. So where are you hiding out? What talent of yours are you not fully supporting? Where are you playing small?

Freedom project: Where are you believing in and investing more in the talent of others than your own talent? Invest in yourself. Believe in yourself. Value yourself and show up with your talent.

20. Recognise that you might be in recovery.

"Recovery is literally covering the ground between your original self and the self you have created and become."

Julia Cameron,
author of *The Artists Way*

Dealing with resistance can be part of our recovery programme. I am sure that you have had the experience of revisiting issues and emotional patterns that you thought you'd handled, but then they come around to be dealt with again but at a higher level. I would often beat myself up for thinking, "I thought I'd dealt with that one." Although I have never been in a formal 12-step recovery programme, I have come to understand that this is part of the recovery process, to revisit old patterns again and gradually they diminish and fade away. So be compassionate with yourself for having to deal with some issues a number of times. We are all in recovery. Don't wait to be a finished item - you are a work in progress.

Freedom project: Which parts of yourself are you recovering? Show up with today's version of your best self, knowing that there will always be more ground to cover and more of you to recover.

Key 2:

The nitty gritty of resistance and how it shows up – know the enemy

The Dalai Lama, the Tibetan Spiritual leader, famously said, "Know your enemy. Your enemy is a good teacher." The enemy is within yourself. To move beyond your resistance successfully and unlock your own potential, it is important to know what resistance is, what it looks like and how it operates. Then, armed with that awareness, you are much more able to move past it. An enemy whose methods are unknown to you is going to be hard to take on, and that is exactly what resistance wants – it thrives on running just outside your awareness. Your blindness to the way resistance works, increases its power over you. It was Martin Luther King Jr. who said, "Love is the only force capable of transforming an enemy to a friend." In a strange way, resistance does you the favour of forcing you to find the best in yourself and bring it forth. Physically just as resistance at the gym helps you create muscle, spiritually, resistance unleashes your capacity for loving and resourcefulness.

So in this section I am going to illuminate many of the ways that I have seen resistance working in my own life and within the lives of the thousands of people I have worked with since 1990.

21. Recognise that there are times when your great intelligence can also be an impediment.

"Your mind can be a great servant but a lousy master."

Anon

A good mind can be a wonderful tool. It can solve problems, operate in the world, make things happen and think clearly. It is also clever at generating fears. Your brain can only understand so much. It only has logic and is only one of many intelligences you have at your disposal. You may pride yourself on knowing the 100 things that could go wrong, of doing a great risk analysis, and seeing the obstacles that could arise. But because you know too much, you execute too little. Sometimes, it takes a leap of faith to get things going. You don't know what is going to emerge into your consciousness. I have rarely figured out in advance how a project was going to succeed, but by moving forward anyway, the path has become clear. If I had used my logic and clear thinking only, I'd still be selling computers.

Freedom project: Recognise when your mind is undermining you and when it is supporting you. Recognise and begin to utilise all the other intelligences you have: physical, emotional, creative and spiritual intelligences.

22. Recognise and relinquish your need to be special.

"Comparison must be an ego device, for love makes none. Specialness always makes comparisons."

A Course in Miracles

We can easily think our issues are different and that we have special forms of resistance, which then builds our ego. Have you read anything here and told yourself, "Yes, but you don't understand my situation/problem/ boss/partner/the demands of my job?"

It's a fundamental ego need to be special. The ego loves to build itself up and specialness is one of its best strategies. You will know that you are doing this if you find yourself saying things like, "My form of resistance is different. That won't work for me. Ah, let me show you why that *doesn't* apply to me. My suffering is unique. My problems are different." The ego builds itself through wanting to be different. It builds itself by aiming to create greater success through competitiveness, and inflation, and by being the best. It can also create specialness by aiming to be the greatest mess, the worst loser and the most insignificant and useless. This is all grandiosity. Another form of specialness is pride – resistance loves pride. When you say, "That's beneath me," resistance loves it. Whether that's taking baby steps, making yourself vulnerable in some way, asking for help or starting again after a successful corporate career, then resistance can kick in and stop you. I am not suggesting for a moment that you demean yourself, but I am suggesting that by taking the occasionally un-sexy but necessary actions, you are likely to succeed much more quickly than by waiting until you are successful enough to have "your people" to do things for you. Tip: What are you refusing to do out of pride? Start doing it. Tip: Accept your shared humanity. Your experience is unique and universal; you are precious and no different.

Freedom project: Acknowledge your shared humanity – you are both unique and very similar to most other human beings. You are influenced as much by resistance as anybody.

23. Over-planning is procrastination in disguise.

"Quit planning your dream and start living it."
Alan Cohen,
Author and Spiritual Teacher

When you are doing what you love, failure is less likely to come from poor planning. It is more likely to come from the timidity to proceed. Sometimes you may find it easier to blame yourself for bad planning, rather than acknowledge your own trepidation. Planning can easily be a form of control that inhibits you and stops you building your confidence by doing what is in front of you now. You can't plan for everything – there are too many unknowns and unknowables – but you can choose to see that as a source of excitement and adventure, rather than fear it.

Freedom project: Dive into the adventure, learn as you go, have your life be the classroom and trust that your soul has a plan that isn't in some glossy folder, but is waiting to unfold within your own heart.

24. Resist the temptation to "just need to know a little bit more" before you start.

"Do everything you can with everything you've got from where you are right now."

Mike Dooley,
Founder of Notes From The Universe

Resistance often whispers to you, "If you had more qualifications and just knew a bit more you'd have more confidence and credibility. So don't start just yet. Get a few more letters after your name." Your fear of not being or knowing enough can often show up as being a perpetual student rather than stepping up and acting on what you already know. It is so tempting to delay by just reading another book, just going on another workshop, just having another coaching session, just getting a few more letters after your name so that you might feel a little more confident and credible. It takes courage and commitment to say, "I know enough to start" and means confronting your own demons and fears. So shift your focus to what you *do* know, the wisdom and knowledge you *do* have and step up and act. You know that you can keep learning forever, but you will grow most by acting on what you already know. There is a big difference between being a voracious learner and a perpetual student. The perpetual student never quite becomes the teacher or leader they could be.

Freedom project: Focus on what you know, and act on what you already know and by all means learn more as you truly need to. Being a voracious learner is about loving learning *and implementing* new ideas, insights and understandings. Always focus on the step you *can* take with who you are *now* and what you know *now*. What is it? Take it!

25. Recognise that resistance can be really nasty.

*"As we move closer to our core, our hidden beliefs that
live in the shadows and secretly call the shots become
exposed. They try to convince the ego to bring out the
heavy artillery and initiate a take-no-prisoners fight to the
finish. What recourse do we have during this dark night
of the soul? Let the ego fight. And while it's distracted with
its business, let's take every opportunity to go within, to go
deeper than ever before, until we're in heaven."*

**Tami Coyne & Karen Weissman,
The Spiritual Chicks**

It is easy to lapse into thinking that resistance really isn't so
bad, that it is just a few unloving and unkind thoughts. You
should not create grandiosity from resistance either, making
it into some unbeatable monster that you feel completely
victimised by. But the reality is that resistance can be very,
very nasty. It will lead you into shame, addictions, self-
destructive and self-sabotaging behaviour. It can take you
to hell. But there are forces in you that are much greater
than resistance. The power of your heart, the pull of love,
your generosity, the desire to serve your fellow brothers
and sisters is greater than resistance. I believe that there are
angels and daimons watching over you, shouting "Grow,
evolve, become!" But you must understand that you
are in a battle, and a battle that you *can* win. When you
underestimate or deny the power of resistance, it can flatten
you and you won't even have seen it coming. So don't be
either too naïve or too cynical – resistance is nasty, but with
awareness, courage, skill and perseverance, you will beat it.

Freedom project: Take resistance both seriously and
lightly. You are in a battle and you can win. But it is a
battle.

26. Don't use your problems and your suffering to define you.

"Who would you be without your story?"

Byron Katie,
Spiritual Teacher and Author of Loving What Is

It is very easy to get attached to problems and the suffering you experience with them and use them as a pillar of your identity. I have done that. I am a depressive, I am ill, I am a loser, I'll never amount to much. Often, in hidden ways, we can be afraid not to have the problem any more. Who would you be without your problems? Your ego is always a mish mash of ideas about who you are, but you may be scared to let them go because you have related to people through your problems. Your problems have served a purpose and can become great excuses not to show up. I used to say to myself, "You can't expect me to show up with the lack of love and encouragement I had growing up…………" Give up the comfort of stories and limits. It can be very easy to argue for our limitations – we can easily be right that we cannot do something and that it is beyond us. But then we don't have to risk, we will just never know. And whilst we won't have made any big mistakes or got anything wrong, we will also know on a deep level that we missed out on the promise of adventure that our own life offered us. Being right about what you can't do is a pale substitute for the experience of deep fulfilment that is on offer. Don't rob yourself of the adventure of realising your own potential.

Freedom project: You actually don't know who you'd be without your problems. Be willing to find out. I think you'll like it. Try on some new identities and see how they might fit for you.

27. Recognise the difference between an obstacle and an excuse.

"Excuses are nothing more than lies that fear have sold you."
Carmen Bell,
South African Entrepreneur

Resistance knows that it can use anything to hold you back. It can easily blur the distinction between a problem and an obstacle. How do you tell the difference? When you are thrown a problem, if you truly want to solve the problem, you will find ways through. You will seek solutions. But I have known many people (myself included), that when you offer them solutions to their problems, are very willing to tell you why that won't work, or will very quickly generate another bigger and juicier problem. The ego pulls out its clipboard and takes great pride in saying, "OK, that was a very good idea, now let me give you 27 very clear reasons why it won't work." The ego needs to be right. When you are inspired you will find a thousand ways to take action, but when you are afraid you will find a thousand excuses. And remember, Lance Armstrong won several Tour de France cycle races while suffering from cancer. Leo Tolstoy had 13 children and still wrote War and Peace (or maybe because he had 13 children!). I am not suggesting for a moment that you berate yourself, but I do want to remind you of what you are capable of when you are truly aligned and inspired.

Freedom project: Be honest with yourself about your fears. Shift from making excuses to being aware and acknowledging your fear and then take a courageous step instead.

28. Give up your worry that you'll be copied.

"Uniqueness is the individual gift that lies within each of us that wants to be expressed. This expression can only come alive through our physical experience. The ultimate purpose of our quest for happiness is to find a way to reconnect to that which makes us unique – this is our gift to our self first, and then to the world."

Aline Hanle, The Quantum Catalyst

Another form of resistance that I see is, people saying to me, "I have a brilliant game changing idea but I can't tell you or anyone else about it in case someone steals it." There can be some truth in that. If necessary, do copyright your ideas and safeguard them. But in my experience, what your ideas need, more than protection, is your active pursuit of bringing them into existence. I had a conversation with a senior executive in publishing a few years ago and she was bemoaning how many authors demanded that she sign a "Non-disclosure agreement", so that she would not share their ideas. She said she usually refused because she knew there were very few life changing ideas that came across her desk. She received hundreds of manuscripts every week so she had a bigger view than most about what was going on. She said that what most authors believed were totally unique ideas were actually very similar to what dozens of other authors were proposing. Being protective can be sensible and mature, but can also become a way of not moving forward because of your fear of being ripped off. Beware of falling into the "specialness trap" and believing that your idea is so special and different and requires special treatment. I know I have been copied and ripped off a few times to my knowledge, and actually I felt quite proud and honoured that something I had done was worth ripping off! I also know that no-one can do your work like you would – it's your uniqueness and no-one can do it like you, even with the same idea. I do believe in a collective consciousness, meaning that if you don't move forward with the idea, someone else will have the idea and if they are more willing to act, you'll miss out and kick yourself and say, "I had that idea." Yes, you may have done – but you need to act. Your success will come from investing more energy in building your idea than waiting for it to be fully protected.

Freedom project: Acknowledge that you can't be copied when you are expressing the unique gifts within you as they are yours and yours alone.

29. Don't leach on the greatness of others – find the greatness in you.

"The hope for humanity is that we may retrieve our shadow from our neighbour."

**Carl Jung,
Swiss psychologist**

By being around other people who are manifesting their greatness in the world, you may hope it will rub off on you. It may, but not because you have taken from them, but because you have found within yourself what you enjoy and admire in them. Let something awaken in you. A great teacher is one who creates more teachers, not more students. The greatest inspiration is the one who creates more inspirers. Let inspiring and great people help you awaken to what is in you, not only what is in them. Meeting others is great – meeting yourself is the best. So all your resistance ultimately is to stop you showing up authentically in the world with what is great in you. There are some gifts you have, some talent you have, some beauty, some love to share with the world, and the whole point of resistance is to stop you showing up. Your fear is that you'll be a disappointment, your strength is not as good as you think it might be, you'll be rejected. So rather than risk the pain, you hide out. But then it's a lose/lose. You are diminished and the world is robbed of you, your talent and your gifts. Resistance allows you to keep your stories running rather than bust through them and show up and find out the actual reality. Tip – so what is the cost of you hiding out and leading a diminished life? Reverse the pain and access your inspiration. Make the pain of hiding out greater than the possible pain of showing up.

Freedom project: Acknowledge that what you admire in others is also in you, maybe hidden or in embryo. Commit to finding the spirit in you, which is no more or no less than anyone else.

30. Other people often serve as the mouthpieces of your unconscious resistance.

"Tell a wise person, or else keep silent, because the mass man will mock it right away."

Johann Wolfgang von *Goethe*, German writer,
Pictorial artist, Biologist,
Theoretical physicist, and Polymath.

I am often asked in talks and workshops, "Yes, this is all OK, but I need to know how I deal with *other people's resistance*." And the honest answer is, "You don't." But what you can do is learn how to respond to others who are themselves in fear and resistance. You can learn not to be de-railed by other people's fears and concerns. Some people are likely to be upset as you beat your resistance. What so often happens is that *their triggers trigger your triggers*. For example, you get all excited about starting your own business and you tell your mother about it and she responds by saying, 'You are thinking about doing *what?* You are thinking of leaving your well-paid and secure job to chase some dream of an idea that you have never tried out? You must be crazy!" You feel crushed and angry, instead of getting support and encouragement, you feel misunderstood, unsupported and angry. And you don't move forward with your dream. Does that dynamic sound familiar to you? You have your fears, others have their fears and when they express their fears, they feed your fears and you go into a downward spiral. It's so easy to pin the blame on others and then you are left feeling powerless. Stop blaming and take responsibility – one of the hardest things to do is to take responsibility for your own resistance. It is so easy to turn other people into the cause of our resistance and problems. Blame causes us to feel a victim, but underneath feeling a victim, is tremendous anger and even aggression. Deep down then we can actually use other people to hold ourselves back, because we are afraid to move forward and show up ourselves. I spent years blaming my Mum for lots of things, "If she had been more loving, affirming, supportive and expressive, I would be very different and could have achieved a lot more." It was horrific when I eventually realised how much I was actually using her, and my resentments of her, as an excuse to not move forward. The more aware we become, the more we can realise how nasty and horrible to ourselves we have been. Stop using others to hold yourself back.

Freedom project: Become skilful at creating a distance between your resistance and the resistance that others may have to your ideas. You are the one with power over your responses. Little by little you can become less reactive and more confident.

31. Forgive yourself your own self-defeating behaviour.

"Greater awareness without greater self compassion can be tough."

Miranda McPherson,
Inter-faith Minister and Author of Boundless Love

As we have discussed earlier, the ego gets you both ways and one of the nastiest areas is around self-defeating behaviour. It usually works something like this: you don't follow through on some opportunity, or you undermine yourself. That's bad enough, as you've robbed yourself of a possibility. But then you go and beat yourself up for not following through or being so stupid, which just reinforces how stupid you are. So you get into a vicious cycle of being harsh on yourself which stops you moving forward, so you feel even worse and the cycle goes on. At the heart of it is obviously the dynamic of self-attack and even self-hatred. The only way through is self forgiveness. Having compassion for yourself, getting yourself off the cross of self crucifixion and back into life. All resistance is a form of self-attack – and the antidote is always self-love and self inclusion and self support. You can only succeed and be happy doing the work you love to the level that you can love and have compassion for yourself. You didn't only start experiencing resistance because you started reading this book. It was always there, but maybe you never really had a name for it, or a language. Use the awarenesses you glean from this book with kindness. As you see what has been hidden, you may recoil a little and be tempted to berate yourself. Instead use it to extend your self compassion. A few years ago I spent a day with some "at risk" youth near Brighton, and one of them, aged sixteen, said to me, "I used to dream when I was younger, but not anymore."

She had written herself off at sixteen. Personally, I believe in a God of new beginnings. Whatever mess we make of life, we are always being offered the opportunity to release the past and make a new start.

Freedom project: Is there a past mistake you are still crucifying yourself for? Ask for help in self-forgiveness. Learn the lesson, integrate the lesson and use it as a foundation to move forward.

32. Understand your grandeur and your grandiosity.

"With the grandeur of God in you, you have chosen to be little and to lament your littleness."

A Course in Miracles

According to *A Course in Miracles* your grandeur is not a statement of pride, but simply a statement of fact. You were created by the Creator as a powerful creator. You are powerful beyond measure. Fact. You cannot change it. Your grandeur is simply waiting to be remembered and awoken to. You have a God-self that cannot be harmed or destroyed but can be hidden or denied. But whatever you do, it awaits your conscious embrace of it. Your grandiosity is of your ego and personality and is how you either inflate or deflate yourself. Either way, it is how you build your ego. To say you are the best in the world (unless you happen to be an Olympic gold medallist) is probably an act of grandiosity. To say that you have no talent, are useless or worthless, are also statements of grandiosity. We all use grandiosity, more often than not to deflate rather than inflate ourselves. Sadly, so many of us get caught in our grandiosity, believing that we are actually being truly humble. It is as if our ego has cleverly switched the signs of grandeur and grandiosity. It says we are grandiose to believe that we have grandeur within us, and that if we show up in our true brilliance, then the ego says we are being arrogant and grandiose.

Freedom project: Accept that there is greatness in you that came with your creation, and that's a fact, not an opinion.

33. Resistance thrives on competition and comparison.

"I really reject that kind of comparison that says, Oh, he is the best. This is the second best. There is no such thing."
Mikhail Baryshnikov, American Dancer

Resistance feeds on getting you to constantly compare yourself with others, usually unfavourably. The key is to look beyond the ego's competition and look into your own heart to see what projects are yours and yours alone. What vision resides in your soul? What promise lies as yet unfulfilled within your own heart? That's where to place your attention – on your own promise and potential. What other people do with their lives is not your problem – living yours truly and fully, is your project.

Freedom project: What is it inside you that wants to emerge and take form? What comparison can you relinquish? Take yourself off 90% of the email lists you are on, if receiving their information makes you feel bad or inadequate.

34. Decide when to call off the search.

"You do not have to seek reality. It will seek you and find you, when you meet its conditions."

A Course in Miracles

There are times to search and explore and research. And then there are times to go deeper with what you have found. One pattern of resistance is to be addicted to searching. Resistance thrives on you keeping all your options open and not committing. One hidden mantra of the ego is *Seek, But Don't Find.* So resistance is very invested in keeping you searching and seeking and very invested in you not finding. Here is the deeper dynamic at work – you are afraid to find your purpose! Your ego doesn't want you to find it, so it will scare you and distract you and keep telling you, "This isn't *quite* the thing for you." This can last your lifetime. I spent years addicted to the search, doubting, creating problems, questioning myself, wondering if this was quite it, whether it could ever work out, doubting whether this thing called purpose even really existed.

Freedom project: Choose something to commit to more deeply. Temporarily go cold turkey on any addiction you might have to searching but not finding.

35. Recognise fights and power struggles as resistance.

"Every fight and power struggle hides your fear of your next step."

Dr Chuck Spezzano,
Spiritual Teacher and Author

Fights and struggles are often a form of resistance. Two years ago I had a situation in my own life where I was in a fight and power struggle for close on four years with a group of people I was involved with. I felt that some of the people involved had reached a plateau, they were stagnating and not evolving. I was in a battle of trying to push them to change. Four years later I was nearly exhausted and gave up the battle. I let go and felt that I had lost the battle. But almost immediately I felt a release of my own creative energy. I wrote my first book in five years. I attracted fabulous new people and opportunities into the vacuum I'd created by letting go. Within 18 months my whole life had leapt to a new level. So much of my energy had gone into pressurising *them* to change, rather than be willing to change myself. Only retrospectively did I really understand that I was afraid of the next step and how good it would be. Indeed, there can be a hidden dynamic beneath each problem – a fear of the next step – problems keep us stuck so we don't have to face even deeper fears, which in turn mask wonderful opportunities.

Freedom project: If you have any battles going on in your life, look at who you are fighting with in your life, and ask, "What is this a distraction from?"

36. Resistance can be building other people's dreams and not investing in your own.

"Regularly check out with yourself and ask, 'Whose dream are you building?'"

Barbara Winter,
Author of Making a Living Without a Job.

You often resist your own dreams by building other people's dreams because you are afraid of building your own dream, and you may not realise you are doing that. When you work for an employer you tend to build their dream, not your own. You may invest in your partner's and family's dreams. You may invest more in your clients' success than your own. Give yourself permission, acknowledge and invest in building your own dream, commission yourself. Investing in yourself is a precious thing to do. I believe there is a healthy selfishness, which is to invest in developing your own God given gifts and talents. They are in you too.

Freedom project: Ask yourself regularly "Whose dream are you building?" Is it the dream in *your* heart? Or someone else's dream?

37. Resistance is the cause of pain, not a protection against pain.

"Resistance is not our enemy. We don't want to push against or 'resist' feeling resistance. What we push against becomes more pronounced in our experience as in, 'what we resist, persists.' What we do want to do with resistance is to ease it, soothe it, reduce it and dissolve it away."

Elyse Hope Killoran in Choosing Prosperity

Resistance is the fear that old pain will re-surface and be experienced again, or that something will happen in the future that will cause pain. And occasionally, that's true. It does take courage to face and feel pain. And sometimes you need to feel the pain in order to allow it to gradually become transformed into a new foundation. The chief pang of most trials is not so much the actual suffering itself as our own spirit of resistance to it. When my Dad died in 2005, I obviously felt a lot of grief. But I felt that there must be something wrong with me that I was in so much pain. I eventually had some bereavement counselling which helped. My big insight was simply this: there was nothing wrong with me, losing someone I loved that much hurt that much. I was afraid to feel that deeply in case I lost myself in the feelings. But when I allowed myself to fully feel the pain rather than resist it, I started to move into new territory and gradually began the process of integration and completion. But it took so much courage. We can transform the pain and use it as fuel rather than avoid it. From time to time, you will get "triggered", meaning that old feelings of shame, grief, rejection, hurt, anger or inadequacy will be stimulated. Often these feelings have very little to do with what is happening in the here and now. They are triggers that have connections to old childhood feelings that you never fully felt then. It can sound tough, but there is often no way around this. Old feelings, in my experience, do get triggered, so don't resist this and allow yourself to feel all the way through until there is a completion. When you have been able to feel something through, you will integrate it and become freer of the fear of it. But today, more than ever, there is help and support and techniques available to help you move through and gently clear yourself from that pain. Find the ones that work for you.

Freedom project: Have the courage to feel deeply, engage with your resistance, push through it, and you will find yourself a little freer and in new territory.

38. Be vigilant to your Master Fear.

"Our Master Fear is that we can succeed, and that we can access the powers we secretly know we possess."
Steven Pressfield in War of Art

What is the Master Fear? I believe it to be the fear of success, of having things be more wonderful and abundant than your limits allow. Your deepest fear is how good it can be, how powerful you are and how bright you can shine. But mostly you hide these fears deep in your mind and may well not even realise that fear. We often feel guilty – guilty that we are more successful than family or friend, and when we feel guilty, there is a part of us which believes that we deserve punishment. Strange as it sounds, deep down we often fear that success might alienate us from others. We will no longer belong in the ways that we did, we will lose love and approval, and it will bring its own set of problems that render its value less than we thought it would be. Or we may fear that this idol of success we were chasing, that we hoped would make us feel so different is actually a disappointment and even fairly meaningless after the initial buzz wears off. It takes courage to be successful – and beware - resistance is more likely to kick in when things hold the potential to get really good for you.

Freedom project: Be a leader in authentic success. Inspire yourself and others by letting your life get really good and feel really good about it. Show us what's possible.

39. Beware of busy-ness and over-enthusiasm.

"Too far, too fast, and we can undo ourselves. Creative recovery is like marathon training. We want to log ten slow miles for every fast mile. This can go against the ego's grain. We want to be great – immediately great – but that is not how recovery works. It is an awkward, tentative, even embarrassing process. There will be times when we don't look good – to ourselves or anyone else. We need to stop demanding that we do. It is impossible to get better and look good at the same time."

Julia Cameron in The Artists Way

Enthusiasm is a tremendous blessing, and the ego is brilliant at taking blessings and turning them into problems. Resistance is happy to get you setting up unachievable goals as a way of sabotaging your success. In my experience, projects always take longer, more energy and are a little harder than you thought. When I was in my early thirties, I went on Tony Robbins workshops, did fire-walks and came away with a long list of goals as long as my arm, so excited was I by the realisation that I needn't be run by old programming and could consciously create my life. Then two weeks later I was depressed because I hadn't achieved them and felt like giving up. My impatience and over-enthusiasm got me and I now realise that it was a form of resistance which then caused me to crash and burn and stop doing what I loved doing. I didn't know that my over-enthusiasm was actually undermining me. Whilst conscious activity builds dreams, excess busy-ness is a great way to avoid your creativity and inner-spirit.

Freedom project: Pace yourself. Think through and get guidance from others about how long something is likely to take. Then decide the realistic duration of the project accordingly.

40. You can live up to your principles to your imperfect best.

"The thing that is really hard, and really amazing, is giving up on being perfect and beginning the work of becoming yourself."

Anna Marie Quindlen,
American author, Journalist and Opinion columnist

Another insidious form of resistance is the fear of not living up to your own ideals, and feeling a fraud, incongruent or even an imposter. Whenever you decide to make a stand for something, there is a good chance your inner critic will chime in and regale you with your own imperfections, inadequacies, flaws and self-judgments. When you are able to be more honest and revealing, then there is less to hide and therefore less to be afraid of. I attended a training course for men called the New Warrior Training adventure run by the Mankind Project. It is an initiation for men whose slogan is "Changing the world one man at a time." In the training they suggest that in every man and woman there is good and there is shadow, there is goodness in every man and there is the undermining and sabotaging of that goodness. This idea helped me a lot. We don't have to be perfect. The invitation is to be open and authentic and aware, to the best of our ability, of our true gifts and what blocks them. I find this liberating. Don't deny or hide your shadow, and neither deny your gold. The gift of maturity is to acknowledge and embrace both.

Freedom project: Acknowledge your gold, your gifts and your love, and also your shadow, your need and your undermining energies. And then please show up with what you do have and with your imperfections too. Be vulnerable enough to be imperfect.

41. Stop looking for short-cuts, and invest your energy into your work.

"The bars of West Hollywood, London and New York are awash with people throwing their lives away in the desperate hope of finding a shortcut, any shortcut. Meanwhile, the competition is at home, working their asses off."

Hugh McLeod, Artist, Cartoonist and Author of
Ignore Everybody* and *39 Other Keys to Creativity

Another form of resistance is looking for short-cuts rather than investing energy into creation and what has meaning for you. The quest for the short cut usually has two elements to it:

1. to find a way of not having to do the work and get straight to the result;

2. to eliminate the risk of failure and go straight to success. Good luck.

I have met so many people who, had they invested the energy they put into trying to find quick fixes and short cuts, into their work instead, they'd probably be massively successful. But instead they invested their energy into short-cutting the work rather than doing the work. I am all for learning from successes and mentors so that you can get to where you want to be by the most direct route. But you still have to travel the path yourself and grow and learn through that journey. Your journey gives you depth. Beautiful things can just happen but usually they emerge from a continuous depth of engagement.

Freedom project: Identify where you are trying to short-cut doing the work and invest in doing the work instead.

Key 3:

Turning pro – the attitude of a spiritual and creative warrior

The idea of being a pro I am using here has nothing to do with being a member of a profession like a lawyer or doctor. It has to do with a mindset, a mindset of being committed to show up and do your work, whatever resistance throws at you. Most of us have already shown some of the skills of being a pro in our work – we show up even when we don't feel like it, we stay because we are being paid. The archetype of the pro is that of the warrior and is not one who loves to fight others, but is the one who does battle with their own inner dragons and demons so that they may bring forth the best of themselves for the benefit of those they lead, love and care for. True warriors serve their God or gods and fight their own dark forces of fear, temptation and apathy. Warriors can be extremely kind. They needn't be scary, but they are committed and focused and know what they stand for in the world. They know that all the real battles are fought within their own hearts and minds, and that is where all the significant victories are too.

As a pro, you develop your skill and ability, you recognise and accept your areas of incompetence and you keep your pipeline to inspiration open. But more than anything else, you simply make a choice: you choose to deliver your work to the world. It is simple but profound: delivering your art is the shoreline where your soul meets the world. You follow through on your inspiration and deliver it to the world, despite the excuses going around in your head, despite the fear in your gut, despite your own doubts. You just go ahead and deliver your gifts to the world, consistently, even and especially when you don't feel like it.

What most motivates you as a pro is to be of service – to be really clear about what you love to share and who you want to share it with. That focus will be your North Star. It will inspire you beyond your resistance to show up with what you have which will brighten the world just one little bit.

As a pro, you are committed to your own inner listening, to serve the gods and hear what their next project for you is. Then you commit to beating your resistance and using your skill to figure out what that idea wants to be in this world and help it come into being. Being a pro doesn't immunise you against fear and problems, indeed, you may even have a few more of them as you commit to your full creative expression. But you are willing because you have tasted the joy of a fully creative life and nothing else fulfils you in the same way.

As a pro you make a commitment to be a servant of the Greater Mystery and as such you learn to start taking success and failure less personally. As you show up for your part of the bargain, commit and invest energy. You know that there are greater forces at work that you can call upon.

42. Turn pro.

"What I call Professionalism someone else might call the Artist's Code or the Warrior's Way. It's an attitude of egolessness and service. The Knights of the Round Table were chaste and self effacing. Yet they duelled dragons."
Steven Pressfield in War of Art

Most of what I am encouraging you to do in this book is to inspire you to turn pro. Being a pro in the context of beating resistance is about making the decision to recognise and beat resistance rather than allow it to beat you. We often think in terms of being an amateur and a pro, where an amateur does something out of love, and a pro does it for the money. Indeed, the Latin root of amateur is amare – to love. But the roots of being a professional derive from "vows taken upon entering a religious order" or "public declaration." In this context, I want to suggest that a professional actually loves their work so much that they want to have it as the centre of their life. So they do it for the love of it, but are also very willing to be paid for it. A true pro says, "I love this so much that I will not let resistance stop me. I choose to battle with my resistance and win so that I can do what I love daily and get paid for doing it."

Freedom project: In what area of your life do you need to turn pro? Please make that commitment to showing up.

43. The pro acts now and invests in anticipation of success.

"Doing anything worthwhile takes forever. Ninety percent of what separates successful people and failed people is time, effort and stamina."

**Hugh McLeod, Artist,
Cartoonist and Author of Ignore Everybody**

As a pro you don't wait for success. You set yourself up by taking the steps that will eventually lead to success. You invest love, time and energy into your work and into developing your skilfulness before any outward sign of success. This investment may take a while but you keep doing it even though there are no guarantees of success and even when you invest in it emotionally. When I met my hero Steven Pressfield, he explained to me that he always dreamed of writing and wrote for many years in deep obscurity. He didn't earn any money from his writing until his 50's and then took even longer to create a good living from it. He is now a million selling author with a Hollywood film made from one of his stories and tremendous respect in the industry.

Freedom project: Commit to developing your artistry and developing your capacity and willingness for success.

44. Quit waiting to be discovered and reveal yourself instead.

"You've got to get up in front of people every day of your life or you'll never learn who you are."

George Carlin,
American Stand-up comedian,
Social critic, Actor and Author

The world can't respond to what you are planning and hoping to do. The world can only respond to you showing up, to your energy, intelligence, enthusiasm, your love and contribution. When you show up, it is generous and comes from your heart and soul, rather than your ego which wants you to think you are showing off. When people witness your love, your gift, they can be touched and they respond. You create a resonance when you show up and you can be found. One of the saddest things is that you have great gifts and those who would be uplifted by them, never get the chance to be, because you are anonymous and invisible to them. Showing off is different – that's about drawing attention to yourself, whilst showing up is actually very generous because then you make your contribution. When you show up you share of yourself and it is extremely attractive.

Freedom project: Where are you hiding out? Show up – let people begin to see and really know you. Show up in some new way every week.

45. Quarantine your drama.

"Drama is a choice. So is peace."

Alan Cohen,
Author and Spiritual Teacher

We all have some drama going on in our lives. Drama can offer temporary excitement and a lift, but it is usually repetitive emotional patterns and behaviour that cause us to feel bad when the excitement wears off. Dramas often have their roots in the places where we felt victimised as children and have still not matured emotionally. Someone saying something to us can trigger that old hook and let out our anger and outrage. Dramas take us over and so distract us, but they are often really unimportant. They are emotional storms that pass quite quickly but can leave us with devastation which can take months to clear up. The positive intent behind dramas is usually a combination of wanting significance and excitement. So shift into positive excitement. Risk. Pioneer. Go to your edge and beyond. That will cause you to grow. That is genuinely exciting. Dramas don't shift things generally. Allow yourself your emotions, but don't dramatise them. The drama is the victim stuff. One of the most powerful ways of shifting from drama is into problem solving and mastery. Invest your energy at getting good at things. It is a different kind of excitement.

Freedom project: Withdraw some of your energy from drama and re-invest it in creativity and building your life. Move from drama to the genuine excitement of growth and problem solving.

46. Remember that relinquishing resistance can be a long-term process.

"It takes a decade to understand the basic nature of spiritual principles, another decade while the ego tries to eat you alive, another decade while it tries to wrestle you to the ground, and finally you begin to walk more or less into the light. Anyone who thinks a spiritual path is an easy one probably hasn't been walking it."

Marianne Williamson,
Author of *The Age of Miracles*.

There is a natural maturing process that happens too – I am now at the age of 53 doing things and being in the world in ways that I dreamed of years ago and at last feel ready enough to be able to do them. It does take time for us to mature, release our fears and build confidence and build mastery. It's not that resistance automatically drops away as we get older. You could be 90 and still be in massive resistance. But as you spend years chipping away at your issues, healing your mind, letting go of old patterns you find a greater inner freedom. Sometimes to me, dealing with resistance feels like the equivalent of drilling through granite: it's making an impact, but the impact is hardly perceptible.

Freedom project: Cut yourself some slack when you are being impatient with yourself. You are like a fine wine taking time to mature.

47. Be scared regularly.

"When people ask me how they can know whether they are on purpose or not, I ask "How frightened are you?" If they aren't afraid, they are probably not on purpose."

Jeff Allen,
Psychology of Vision Master Trainer

As a pro, if you are not regularly scared, you are probably playing too safe. It's part of the job description for being an inspired and creative soul that you need to take yourself to the edges of your discomfort. That is how you stretch, grow and become more of who you are in essence. Move towards the new work that thrills, excites and scares you.

Freedom project: Your fear is a sign of your growth – consciously move towards your fear. Pick the fear you need to move towards next and take steps into that fear.

48. Recognise the difference between the suffering ethic and birth pains.

"We must be willing to get rid of the life we've planned, so as to have the life that is awaiting us.... The old skin has to be shed before the new one is to come."

Joseph Campbell, Mythologist

Growth can be joyous and graceful at times, and painful at other times. Most mothers say that childbirth is painful but they soon shift into the joy of parenting. Very few mothers are still blaming their children for that pain years later. The same with resistance. We can get in the old suffering ethic that says, as long as there is pain, sacrifice, difficulty and distress involved, then that is good for the soul and makes us righteous and good people. Or we can recognise that there is suffering in life, but that is not the purpose of life. Suffering need not identify you. No more martyrs are required. You are called to live fully. Being human involves suffering but suffering doesn't make us any more loveable or valuable. Maybe this tip doesn't apply to you, but I have certainly had what has seemed like my own addiction to suffering, putting myself through a lot of it, in the hope that it would make me a better person. I now know that this has been part of an erroneous belief that suffering makes me a better human being, coupled with a belief that God wants me to suffer. I now know that this is not true. And I also know that my suffering has broken me open to greater compassion for myself and others.

Freedom project: Identify your belief in the need to suffer and whether you might believe that your suffering will redeem you.

49. Master your ego.

*"The happiness of a man in this life does not consist in
the absence but in the mastery of his passions."*

Alfred, Lord Tennyson,
Victorian Poet Laureate

Some people have the goal of eliminating their ego and
trying to get rid of it. Good luck.

My suggestion is, instead of eliminating your ego, accept it
and allow it, and make mastery of it your goal. Let your ego
serve your soul and align with it. Resistance only comes
from your ego, and this is the negative side of ego. Fighting
it only strengthens it. Instead strengthen that professional
core of you, that part of you that is greater than your ego.
You need an ego to operate in this world, to carry out tasks,
to structure things, to hold your own and help you remain
sovereign. Your ego can be a marvellous servant to your
heart and your spiritual purpose. You can receive inspiration
and then know how to act, to create your book, your
enterprise, your programme, your school. We need both
heart and mind. I remember a conversation I had nearly
twenty years ago in Samye Ling, a Buddhist monastery in
Lockerbie, Scotland with a Lama there. I felt intimidated
when he asked me, "And what do you do?" and trying to
think of something worthy to say, I responded with, "Oh,
I am trying to bring spirit into business." He smiled and
responded by saying, "That's interesting, we are trying to
bring business into spirit!" He went on to explain how
they were great meditators and had great understanding
of the mind and awareness, but were grappling with cash-
flow, marketing, PR and operational management in a
new country after leaving Tibet. For me the hardest things
are accepting my own "negative" ego traits like jealousy,

pettiness, anger and frustration. I still struggle to accept that as a human being I have all those negative qualities whilst still being the owner of a magnificent soul.

Freedom project: Master your ego and let it serve your soul, and let your soul serve the Divine.

50. Work for love first – and be very willing to be paid.

"At the beginning of my career as an artist in the 1960's, I only set up one dictum for myself: I didn't want to work for pay, but I did want to be paid for my work."
Leonard Cohen, Poet, Singer and Songwriter.

The primary motivation for your creative work and your contribution needs to be love and to uplift the lives of your fellow human beings. You must love the work, want to share your gift and your love, and you must love doing it for the intrinsic fulfilment you experience, for the feeling of personal alignment and rightness you feel. The feeling of making good on your promise and knowing the life you are living is your own authentic life is second to none, this side of Heaven. Let your guiding dictum also be to work for love first, do what you love and share your gift. And at the same time be very intelligent about how you can get paid and be very willing to be paid. It can be easy to edit, adapt and change what we would love to do in order to be liked, approved of, loved, make more money or not offend anybody. But it is that spark of love and authenticity that is actually attractive. When you do it for love, for the adventure, as service and to serve your gods, it has a different feel to it. It is seen and felt as a gift rather than as a marketing strategy. Then people respond differently. An open heart is the best market strategy there is.

Freedom project: Work for love first and foremost because people will respond to your love – and be intelligent and willing to be paid.

51. Sometimes, act in faith and in anticipation of inspiration.

"The only limits to our realization of tomorrow will be our doubts of today. Let us move forward with strong and active faith."

Franklin D. Roosevelt, Former US President

You don't always feel like doing what you do – but you get into the flow by engaging with your work and just doing it. You need to understand that inspiration can be constantly available to you, but you have to engage with your work to trigger the flow of that inspiration. Don't wait for inspiration to strike you. You can initiate the flow by taking the steps. I found one of the hardest aspects of living an inspired life to be, how to live with myself when I don't feel that inspired. I can be prone to all sorts of negativity when I am out of the flow of inspiration. Do your work and you will initiate the flow of inspiration, sometimes immediately and sometimes it takes time.

Freedom project: Stop waiting until you really feel like it, and start doing your work, and you will initiate the flow of inspiration and ideas and energy. Initiate the process of getting into flow and of emergence.

52. Recognise it's all fear.

"Every decision is a choice between love and fear."
A Course in Miracles

As a true pro, the realisation dawns on you that all your resistance, however cleverly disguised it is, however cunning and well wrapped it appears, is nothing more than fear. All your excuses are just excuses. You can remove all the masks and see that there is only one dynamic in them – fear. Gradually, as you allow yourself to acknowledge your own fear for what it is, you can own it for what it is without shaming yourself for it. There are only ever two choices: if it is not love and creative expression then it is fear, however it may look.

Freedom project: Accept your fear, stop treasuring your excuses and show up.

53. Trust your own uniqueness and don't try to copy others.

"The creation of an individual is a divine masterpiece. We were dreamed for a long time before we were born. Our souls, minds and hearts were fashioned in the imagination. Such care and attention went into the creation of each person. Given the uniqueness of each of us, it should not be surprising that one of the greatest challenges is to inhabit our own individuality and to discover which life-form best expresses it."

John O'Donohue in Benedictus

Trying to be unique can be another neurotic pursuit – be authentic and inhabit yourself fully - that will make you unique. One of the greatest gifts you can give life is to inhabit your own unique corner of creation and to be authentically yourself. That is what the world is hungry for, the world doesn't want anyone else trying to impress us, or compete with us. The world is hungry for more authentic brilliance. Learn to value and recognise and celebrate your own uniqueness, and the literal fact that no-one on this planet has the unique values, insights, experiences and gifts that you do. On one of my programmes, I do an exercise where I get people into groups of four and each person takes it in turn to stand in the middle of their circle and talk about "Inspiration." Given only one minute to talk about one word, all the participants are amazed to see how they each have a different take on inspiration, different passions and different insights. So trust that your unique take has value. Another way I have come to describe this is this: most of us are concerned with similar subjects – love, inspiration, dreams, authenticity, successfully being ourselves, beating our fears and insecurities, making money, having a good life. These are universal ideas and you are a unique expression of these universal ideas. And there are people hungry to hear your take on life with your unique insights.

Freedom project: Embrace the truth that you are a precious and unique corner of creation. All of evolution has led to you. You are made of star dust and sunshine.

54. Be willing to invest your energy in projects with unknown outcomes.

"The only guarantees in life are death and taxes."
Arnold Patent, Author and Teacher

You can't demand success, you can only do your work in faith and surrender its results to a greater intelligence. So many people say to me, "When I can be sure my book will be a best-seller, I will get on and write it. When I know my enterprise will be a success, I will launch it." There is a part in each of us that is understandably looking for a guarantee of success. That's natural. But in truth, there are very few guarantees of success in life. Companies with billions in turnover still launch products and services that fail. But instead of thinking, "So what hope is there for me?" be inspired to think you are actually in a fantastic position to try things out without investing millions. You need to be willing to invest energy so that you can learn, grow and discover. The Hindu scripture *Bhagavad-Gita* tells us we have a right only to labour, not to the fruits of our labour. All you can do as a warrior is to give your all and surrender your work for a higher power.

Freedom project: Where do you need to proceed in faith? Proceed.

55. When delaying tactics are no longer working, resistance goes for your jugular.

"Your inner critic is often loudest when you are at the creative best."

Julia Cameron,
Author of the Artists Way

The ego's most common form of resistance is procrastination. That's enough to stop most of us. But when you get more inspired, more wilful and connect to your higher purpose and start to confront your procrastination, the ego then pulls out its bigger guns. It starts questioning your very character and integrity. It gets you believing that there is something wrong with you. You must be stupid or dumb. You start feeling bad about yourself. Old shame can arise. The ego aims to get you to believe that you are fundamentally flawed, even evil and sinful. So don't underestimate resistance. It aims to kill your character.

Freedom project: There is nothing wrong with you, however much resistance you might be experiencing. You are growing.

56. You do need to feel safe but not in the way resistance tells you.

"If you knew who walked beside you on the journey you have chosen, fear would be impossible."

A Course in Miracles

Resistance can speak in a voice that seems to make a lot of sense. Don't put yourself out there because it could be very painful. You could be rejected, criticised, humiliated attacked and judged and end up feeling terrible. So it does *appear* to be your friend, saving you from potential pain. And of course, you don't want to be reckless and expose yourself to unnecessary pain. So where does that leave you? You play safe, but feel unfulfilled. You were born to fly and to blossom. There is an unconditional self in you that has always been safe. Trust the voice in you that is calling you to blossom, to show up and recognise that your safety comes from within you, not from things around you.

Freedom project: Remember your safety comes from finding what is in you, that is greater than your fear. There is a place in you that is completely safe.

57. Don't invest too much of your identity in what you do.

"The purpose of life is for the individual to become greater than the definitions he has inherited."

**James Baldwin, American novelist,
Essayist, Playwright, Poet, and Civil rights activist.**

One form of resistance is investing too much of your personal identity in your projects. When your own sense of self and self worth is too heavily tied up in the success of your projects, you can easily lose your sense of freedom in what you are doing. You do what you think will achieve results rather than what is in your heart to do. You don't put stuff out in case it fails, you edit what you do and you feel crushed when things go wrong. You are bigger than your projects. You are a precious, innately valuable corner of creation regardless of your achievements. You will continue to live, eat and breathe beyond all successes and failures. There are many works in you to exist over your lifetime. Don't get too hooked up on any of them. The more you have over invested emotionally in the project, the more resistance can feed. So the answer is to be at the same time both wholehearted and healthily detached. Invest your love and energy, but not your whole identity. Find that professional core within you.

Freedom project: Remind yourself that your being is greater than all your projects combined. The source is within you and is infinite.

58. Demystify inspiration.

"That talk of inspiration is sheer nonsense; there is no such thing. It is a mere matter of craftsmanship."
**William Morris, English textile designer,
Artist, Writer, and Socialist**

Obviously, I don't completely agree with the quote by William Morris, but it is true that for your work to be wonderful, there needs to be craft and technique too. Success does not come from being in an intoxicated state of inspiration 24/7, but it is the initial spark of inspiration that makes it exciting and meaningful. You can come up with any explanation for inspiration that you like - angels whispering in your ear; a muse that sprinkles magic dust on you and your projects; your unconscious mind popping into your consciousness; God revealing to you. In truth no-one can be sure what inspiration is, no-one can tell you where an idea was before it popped into your mind. What you can be sure of is that you can rely on the process. You'll always have ideas and inspiration. So don't spend too much time questioning the source or wondering about the source. It is an awesome thought, but don't be overawed by it. The pro knows that they can get caught up in the mystery, but they also know that they have a job to do and works to bring into existence.

Know that your job is three fold:

- to listen and receive;

- to beat resistance and inertia;

- to act to create.

You often hear creative people saying something like, "I don't know what my next idea is or even if I'll have another great idea." But they know in their hearts, they will, but they can't predict when or how it will happen. All they can be pretty sure of is that, as they commit to engaging with their work and being in the flow, then new insights and inspiration will emerge into their consciousnesses. By doing their work, the magic keeps coming. I also hear many people say, "I have so many ideas, I don't know where to start." Start with the ones that most excite you and scare you a bit too.

Freedom project: Don't worry about the future so much. Do what you are inspired to do right now. The next step of inspiration will follow as you complete the steps in front of you now. It's lovely to fall in love with ideas and their possibilities and plan what your idea could become. It takes courage and energy to actually take action and find out.

59. Sometimes resistance just wants to take you out.

"Sometimes it seems that the only way to end the pain or exhaustion is death. This is invitation to a new birth in your life and to truly choose life."

Dr Chuck Spezanno
Spiritual Teacher and Author

There may be times, there certainly have been for me, when resistance either whispers or shouts, "Just give up on yourself. You'll never make it. Just die." There have certainly been times when the steps I have been taking have seemed futile in relation to the size of the dream in my heart. I felt like the mountain to climb was just too high, the distance to cover too great. I just felt like I should end it all. But of course, when you hit rock bottom, if you can stick with it, the only way is up. In those situations, the best advice I can give is this: Keep dreaming, hold onto your vision. Keep taking baby steps. Keep trusting yourself and the power of transformation. Three years ago I discovered my personality type in the Enneagram, an ancient system of personality profiling. I was a type four, and this is how I was described: "Deep-sea diver of the human psyche: you delve into the inner world of the human soul and return to the surface, reporting on what you found. You are able to communicate subtle truths about the human condition in ways that are profound, beautiful and affecting. In fundamental ways, you remind us about deepest humanity – that which is most personal, hidden, and precious about all of us but which is, paradoxically, also the most universal." If that resonates with you at all, then maybe you too are someone who goes to their depths to find a gift for yourself and everyone. The ego can invite you into a death temptation, but understand that it is you regaining another little piece of your soul and a gift to you and everyone. You have the courage to make the world a little safer for everyone in it, and to help take away some of people's fears. You can face your darkest fears and liberate yourself from them.

Freedom project: However far down you might go, you can come up again. Nowhere is unreachable for grace. Be willing to shed a skin and have a new chapter of life.

60. As a pro, you like to keep things simple.

"Contrary to what some may believe, simplifying is not about retreating to a cabin in the woods and leading a dull, inactive existence. Rather, cutting back your hectic work pace gives you the opportunity to make sure that you're doing work you love. If you're not, you can change what you do."

Elaine St. James, Simplicity Guru

In a world of complexity, the pro aims to keep an eye on the few things that are truly important. The pro is looking to learn how to achieve success without stress and overwork. Simplifying offers a gateway to a rich and rewarding inner life. Having that inner connection will make it so much easier to move beyond society's demands and expectations about work. When I was younger, I prided myself on how much I could take on, whilst today I am more proud of myself for what I can say no to. With so many choices and decisions, so many demands from people and events, in our modern fast changing world, it's a real challenge to 'keep it simple'. Making it simple means making things easy and clear. The magic wand to wave over your life is prioritising and then planning your life around your priorities. The simplification of life is one of the steps to inner peace.

Freedom project: What can you simplify today - your desk, perhaps your thoughts, a meeting? Simple means easy. Simple means asking, "Is this really necessary?"

Key 4:

The professional's tool kit - strategies to get beyond resistance

You beat your resistance through a combination of your awareness, your intention and mindset and practical strategies. In essence, you get through resistance by a choice – of making something else more important than fear. And you can support those choices with tools and strategies. You need your full repertoire of mind, heart and spirit to beat your resistance. It was John Ruskin who said, "When love and skilfulness come together, expect a masterpiece." He got it spot on. Skill with love is clever and efficient. Love without skill can be less effective. The two together create a mighty marriage of head and heart and when fuelled by the spirit within you, you can and will beat your resistance.

61. Choose to be of service to life.

"A business absolutely devoted to service will have only one worry about profits. They will be embarrassingly large."

Henry Ford,
Founder of Ford Motor Company

To keep going through the times of fear and discomfort you are likely to experience, you need to have your heart set on some greater horizon, some higher purpose. That is what is going to get you through the time when it is tempting to give up and give in to the voices of fear, doubt and conformity. What will you make more important than your own fear? At some point I know I made a transition. I know that so many people had inspired and influenced me, and I know how much poorer my life would have been if they had not shown up by giving in to their resistance. I had begun to receive some good feedback for what I was doing, but also found myself regularly caught by resistance and self-doubt. So I made a decision, not very consciously and quite clumsily, but I made it: to make showing up and making my contribution more important than feeling crap about myself. If I could make a difference to someone else, as so many had made a difference to me, then I would commit to doing that. The best way through resistance and self-consciousness is to be in service.

Freedom project: Make a choice to see beyond your own self-consciousness and look and ask "Who needs your help?" By extending yourself, you will feel better about yourself.

62. Start *before* you feel ready.

"I've never begun any important venture for which I felt adequately prepared."

Sheldon Kopp,
Psychotherapist and Author

The idea of maximal preparation before you start is largely a myth. You become prepared by engaging with and doing your work. You become ready through having the courage to do the thing you have come here to do. You can express this in many ways: you don't get wet thinking about water; you don't become a great chef by studying recipe books; you don't become a good driver by studying the highway code. You grow in confidence and ability, learn and mature by engaging with your work, not by planning to.

Freedom project: Always remember that your best time to start is before you are ready. Start a project you keep procrastinating about because you haven't felt ready. Pluck up your courage.

63. Learn to feed your inspiration and starve your resistance.

"If you gave your inner genius as much credence as your inner critic, you would be light years ahead of where you now stand."

Alan Cohen,
Author and Spiritual Teacher

Invest in your inspiration, energy, aliveness and possibility and invest less energy in feeding and magnifying your fears. Watch less TV, media and news that speak of hopelessness, doom and fear. Read and watch and listen to more that uplifts your heart, nourishes your spirit and adds to the love in you. Read amazing stories of amazing people that inspire you and remind you of what you are capable. Spend time with loving and encouraging people who see the beauty of you and your dreams and want to see you succeed and are willing to help where they can. Be with people who have overcome their fears and problems so that they give you hope and practical advice. Your resistance will always point you at the evidence to support your fear and sense of limitation. You do need to develop the discipline to notice that and make new decisions on where to place your focus and attention.

Freedom project: Spend time every week at your three most significant wells of inspiration doing what most feeds you and uplifts your soul.

64. Give yourself permission to make mistakes and to learn and still be OK.

"Mistakes are the portals of discovery."

James Joyce,
Irish novelist and Poet

I meet so many people who say to me, "Whatever I do next, I must GET IT RIGHT! I have too many cul-de-sacs, this has got to be right and it must work. I have got to figure it out properly." That's an awfully heavy burden for a project or goal to carry, and for you to carry. Somehow they want to by-pass the growth pains, the risk, the adventure, the learning and growth, and fast-forward to guaranteed success. This hides the fear of failure, getting it wrong and looking stupid. You must allow yourself to make mistakes, to explore, to experiment and to succeed, fail and learn. Most people's fear of failure shows up as not even starting so they don't put themselves in a position where they could fail.

Freedom project: Please shift from punishment to correction and to learning. Please shift from getting it right to adventure and allowing yourself to learn. You only learn by doing, so get going and learn from your success and your mistakes. And be kind to yourself, please.

65. Embrace your fear of people being jealous of you.

"To some people your example will give them hope but some people will be envious and jealous, making them even more aware of their own issues and inadequacies. And maybe it's easier for them to attack you than their own demons."

Hugh McLeod, Artist, Cartoonist and Author of
Evil Plans – Having Fun on the Road to World Domination

Here is the deal – the more successful you become, the more jealousy you could attract. Some people may try to diminish you because you have had the boldness and courage to do what they didn't have the courage to do. You remind them of their own passivity, their own feelings of inadequacy, and even their cowardice. And instead of thanking you for helping them, become aware of issues they need to deal with, they attack and blame you instead. Your happiness may trigger their suffering. They will feel uncomfortable and they will try to pin that on you to make you feel bad like they do. Your job is to clear your own guilt and feel OK about your success. See where you have guilt, fear and unworthiness and clear it out. Your true happiness and success are actually leadership qualities and can inspire others.

Freedom project: Recognise that jealousy from others is your ego telling you that you can't have good things yourself. You can. Know that deep inside you have everything you need to be happy and successful. Discover the place in you that is free of guilt and judgement – your innocence.

66. Give yourself fully and hold nothing back.

"Give to the world the best you have, and the best will come back to you."

Ella Wheeler Wilcox,
Poet and Journalist

The ego will always tell you that your safety is achieved through withholding and holding back. It tells you that when you don't give and extend yourself, you cannot be rejected. But the very quality you hold back from sharing, is the thing that would make the difference and could create your success. The more you put your heart out there, the more you will create success.

Freedom project: Give a little more of yourself than you would normally – but true giving from your heart, not from sacrifice.

67. Bust the myth that successful people obviously don't have resistance.

"When I started sending out Notes From The Universe, I felt so arrogant, who did I think I was? I was so scared and full of doubt."

Mike Dooley,
Founder of Notes From the Universe

Twenty five years ago, when I was creatively blocked, I would look at creatively and entrepreneurially successful people and say to myself, "They obviously don't understand my struggles. It's all right for them. If they had my upbringing, then they wouldn't be able to do what they do." I think I prided myself that my own problems were unique and special and didn't allow me to fly like others seemed to. It's only as I have become more functional myself that I can see that most people I admire have not led struggle and resistance free lives. They have overcome their own fears, obstacles and challenges. Today, I like to think I am a little less jealous and a little more humble. I recently interviewed Mike Dooley, New York Times best-selling author and founder of the *Notes From The Universe*. He is one of the most successful messengers of metaphysical ideas on the planet. Previously an accountant, he left to set up a tee-shirt business with his brother and mother, which then folded, and he was left with a big mortgage a few names on an e-mail address list and a life-long interest in spiritual and metaphysical principles. He described feeling lost and quite terrified, but felt a call to start sharing inspiring ideas with people, and got a positive response. Eventually he was inspired to create notes signed from *The Universe* and again he judged his audacity very harshly but just putting one step in front of another, he started to get interest, offers of speaking, and his business grew little by little from there. Today, his notes go out to 400,000 daily, he has a massively successful business and is in demand to speak around the planet. But it only came from his own willingness to move forward in inspiration in the face of his own fears, doubts, self-judgement and insecurity. His success has been on the other side of massive resistance.

Freedom project: Read some of the "early days" stories of the people you admire. Discover their challenges and resistance so you can re-assure yourself that there is nothing wrong with you and that you can beat your resistance.

68. Exercise your creative muscles every way you can.

"The more creativity you use, the more you have."
Maya Angelou, Poet, Educator, Historian,
Best-selling author, Actress, Playwright,
Civil-rights activist, Producer and Director

In February 2011, I attended a two day Creativity Boot
Camp in London with Julia Cameron. On day one, someone
asked me, "Why are you here if you've already written six
books?" I had to think for a minute before I could realise that
my answer was, "I have written six books *because* I keep
attending events like this." During that event, so many ideas,
impulses and forces awoke within me. I am still feeling the
ripple effect months later and this book is one consequence
of me attending that event. I encourage you to be creative in
any and all areas of your life because it will have a positive
impact on all areas of you and your life. I once ran two
workshops in a beautiful town called Cadaques in Northern
Spain where both Pablo Picasso and Salvador Dali had
lived. I visited Dali's home which had been re-created as
a museum, and was struck by how many experiments of
creativity were there. I knew Dali as a painter, but there
were bits of tin foil and pieces of rubbish he had turned into
sculptures, sketches, pieces of furniture. I felt deeply that
Dali just kept having inner impulses and he didn't censor
himself, he just played and experimented and didn't judge
himself. He had given himself creative freedom to express
himself. I had grown up learning how to censor and stop
myself, and this possibility touched something in me.

Freedom project: Regularly expose yourself to the
creativity of others and immerse yourself in as much of
the creative expression of others as you can. Ask yourself
what canvass can you express yourself on next.

69. Be willing to die and be reborn.

"And so long as you haven't experienced this: To die, and so to grow, you are only a troubled guest on the dark earth."
Johann Wolfgang von Goethe, German writer, Pictorial artist, Biologist, Theoretical physicist, and Polymath

Now that can obviously sound a little dramatic but then life is a series of deaths and of letting go so that new life can emerge. Resistance is often holding on to outdated and outmoded ideas about yourself. Every temptation to death is actually an invitation to a new chapter of your life. Resistance can be hitting the wall of some fossilised belief, attitude or idea that needs to die so that something new can emerge. So, have many incarnations in a lifetime – often resistance is about holding onto to some idea or project and trying to milk it beyond its sell by date. There are many works of art, ideas, businesses and inspired projects. When you hold on to any for too long and don't evolve either the existing project or onto the next project, then you become stuck. Transformation is possible, and often you have to let go and grieve before the new can arrive. I don't know whether re-incarnation is true or not. What I do know though is that, at age 53, I feel like I have already been through several incarnations in this one life. That's all that really matters. Allow the old to die away so that the new can emerge. Be re-born, in this life, don't wait for the next.

Freedom project: What needs to die within you? What do you need to let go of? What wants to be born in you? Consider a ritual to symbolically let it go and invite in the new.

70. It is usually not about the money.

"Humans have created a disconnect between "doing good" and being well compensated. On the other hand, doing things of somewhat less lasting and intrinsic value can produce compensation in the millions. Thus, society values discourage noble actions and encourage triviality and illegality. Humanity's watchword is: The higher the purpose, the lower the reward."

Neale Donald Walsch,
Author of *Conversations with God*

I can't and won't make money doing that, is one of the ego's cleverest strategies for stimulating your fear and keeping you where you are. And I know how scary that is. Staying on a conventional career path, earning money, doing a job for someone else has been largely how the world has been set up for generations. Your ego tells you that wandering off that straight and narrow path is career and financial suicide. In the space of a generation now, the world of work and careers is transforming. *I can't make money doing that* is one of the most self-betraying things you can tell yourself. Today, the world has never been so full of opportunities for you to make your living doing something you love doing. But your resistance could easily have you staying where you are rather than ploughing your own path and generating income from what you love doing. I have started a project called, "You get paid to do what?" in which I share amazing ways that people earn money today. One story I tell in my seminars is of a woman I met and when I asked her what she did for a living, she replied, "I get paid to be massaged." Obviously a bit thrown, I enquired further and she explained that one of her jobs was teaching massage and that she had to receive massages so that she could verify the competence of the students!

Here are a few other examples and I would love you tell me about others you know and get to hear about:

- **Beers stylist.** My partner Helen was recently on the set as part of making an advert for a lager (The one that reaches the parts others don't reach) and she got chatting to one of the guys. When she asked him what his job was, he replied "I am a beer stylist – it's my job to make the beer look as good as possible on camera!"

- **Skidding friction testers.** Watching TV recently there was a documentary on Edmonton airport in Canada and how they keep it open during their harsh winters. They have a team of people whose job it is to drive cars along the runways and to keep skidding. The cars have onboard equipment that measures the friction of the skid and when it drops below a certain level it is dangerous for planes to land so they bring in the snowploughs.

- **Watching films.** My friend Brian gets paid as a film critic and so is paid to go to cinema to watch films and also to stay at home and watch DVDs

- **Making moustaches and wigs** At a lunch party recently I met the woman who runs a business making many of the wigs and moustaches for films, and the Harry Potter films had been keeping her very busy

- **Eating and sleeping** My cousin Jackie is a hotel inspector - her job is to anonymously go to bed and breakfast places, eat their food, drink their wine, stay in their bedrooms and then produce a report afterwards to tell them how they can improve their service

Freedom project: Allow yourself to imagine what you would most love to be paid for doing or being. Capture those ideas. Start thinking about how you could get paid and take small steps.

71. Show up for your part of the deal.

"I say to the Muse, "I am showing up for my part of the deal – you better show up with yours." I am going to show up anyway, because that is my job. I want the record to show that today I showed up for my part of the job."
Elizabeth Gilbert, Author of *Eat, Pray, Love*

Magic and often miracles follow when you show up but your ego will always tell you that it is unsafe to shine and show up. Resistance will always tell you that being visible, successful and happy are somehow unsafe. But actually, showing up is one of the keys to beating resistance. Whether it is showing up to your computer to write, showing up in your office, showing up in front of people, showing up opens the doors to inspiration, relationships and success. When you are inspired to do something, have an intuition or a hunch about something, show up and follow through and see what opportunity might be waiting. I could literally tell you hundreds of stories about what has happened when I have shown up, and when clients have shown up. I do believe that hidden forces and hands are at work nudging us along and orchestrating situations and events and the mechanism by which much of that happens is through us showing up.

Freedom project: You can never know what will happen as a result of you showing up – so you show up for your part and let the magic begin.

72. Understand it is baby steps all the way.

"A question to ask yourself each morning, that really lights fires, gongs bells, and summons resources is, "What little, mortal, baby steps can I take today that will demonstrate expectancy, prepare for my dream's manifestation, and above all, place me within reach of life's magic?" Please, ask this question, and then answer it with those little, baby steps, even when they're sometimes the same steps you took yesterday. I promise you, you'll go down in history as a giant among your kind. It's never too late."

Mike Dooley, Notes from the Universe

You may well get inspired with a grand vision, know how you want your life to change, and then wonder, "And how am I ever going to get there?" and your heart can sink. Baby steps are one of the most magical things in the universe. Learn to celebrate every step you take and every victory you have over resistance. You can achieve pretty much anything by putting one foot in front of the other and keeping moving. You can write books, create successful businesses, lose weight, build loving relationships, make a million and find inner peace, all by taking baby steps. Resistance will tell you that baby steps aren't sexy, they don't work, and they aren't worth taking because they won't take you to where you want to go. Your pride can kick in big time and tell you that baby steps are beneath you. But whatever your long-term goal, it is baby steps all the way. Don't confuse taking baby steps with acting small, though. Baby steps prepare you for success, while acting small keeps you afraid and sets you up for failure. Baby steps can feel silly, but they also demonstrate how badly you want what you want.

Baby steps set you up for miracles, breakthroughs and quantum leaps along the way too, and they'll all come about because you've been taking the baby steps. Each step will move you forward, you'll learn something, get insights and make connections.

Freedom project: Take baby steps all day every day – start and keep doing the damn thing!

73. You learn the "how to" do it as you go.

"Learning is what most adults will do for a living in the 21st century."

**Sidney Joseph Perelman, Humorist,
Author and Screenwriter**

This is what Mike Dooley calls the cursed hows. You can't know. It is not a case a case of "OK, I finished my education when I left school and now all I need to do is apply what I learned and I will succeed." You have started knowing that you don't know it all, and you don't even know what you don't know. It *is* an act of faith. When I left my corporate job I knew vaguely where I wanted to get to. I have moved in that direction consistently. I have had some spectacular results – but did I know precisely how they were going to happen? Never. And still don't. I can only assume – or know – that there are unseen hands at work. The brain and conscious mind only has a limited view of things. It cannot see the big picture. Only greater intelligence can see that. But life is responsive rather than unresponsive.

Freedom project: Move in the general direction of your heart. You don't have to have clarity about the details. Your path *will* come clear as you walk it.

74. Even when resistance feels awful, you can move through it.

"All of the significant battles are waged within the self."
Sheldon Kopp,
Psychotherapist and Author

Even the tiniest of steps that feel pathetic can help get you through. Often I have written with tears streaming down my cheeks. Resistance is actually a celebration and acknowledgment and symptom of growth and your courage to feel deeply. You can feel awful and still act. When you grow, sometimes it is easy, sometimes it is painful. You can feel all your feelings and still show up in the world. There have been times when I have felt so scared and vulnerable as I am about to stand up to give a talk and yet within minutes of starting to speak, I am in my flow and am uplifted into the jet-stream of inspiration. But it can take incredible courage to feel so bad and still show up. But you have that courage within you.

Freedom project: Be willing to feel more fully, knowing that even your worst feelings won't last forever.

75. Now is always a good time.

"First rule of decision making: More time does not create better decisions. In fact, it usually decreases the quality of the decision. More information may help. More time without more information just creates anxiety, not insight."
Seth Godin, Author

Procrastination will always have you believing that now is not quite the right time to make decisions and act, and that you need to be different from who you are. It will tell you that the economy needs to pick up first, your kids need to grow up more or you need to get more education. It will also tell you that you need to know more, be more and have more before you can proceed. But there is always something you can do and be now, today. Better to make some decisions today and then adjust course, rather than wait to make perfect decisions one day.

Freedom project: So ask yourself each day: What *can* I do today? What decisions will I make today? What *do* I know today? What resources *do* I have today? What courage *do* I have today?

76. Break your isolation.

*"Like many entrepreneurs, I go to Starbucks a lot.
But not for the coffee. I go there because I'm lonely. I
go there because I crave human interaction. I go there
because I need to talk to real people every day. Being an
entrepreneur is bloody lonely."*

**Scott Ginsberg,
Author and Teacher**

Resistance breeds on your isolation. Community,
friendship and accountability break that isolation. In
a recent workshop, Judy described how lonely she
felt – she loved her work and enjoyed running her own
business but lived alone and felt terribly isolated. Her
resistance was breeding like mushrooms in the darkness
of that isolation. A few hours in the company of the
group and a few tears later and she was a different
woman. I still say that a couple of days working on my
own at home and I find myself "behind enemy lines."
My demons surface, the gremlins come out of the
woodwork and I can begin to dislike and doubt myself
and lose my confidence. People offer us mirrors, they
reflect back to us our goodness and strength and that we
are OK, liked and loveable. So get phenomenal support
and accountability in your life – one of the greatest
myths I had for many years at the beginning of my own
business was this: that doing my own thing meant doing
it alone. I believed that isolation and loneliness were
the price I had to pay for ploughing my own path in life.
Wrong! Doing your own thing is a fabulous invitation to
be with those who feed your soul. To love and support
and encourage each other. To care for each other. To
celebrate and commiserate together. To share ideas and
resources. Surround yourself with kindred spirits. Who

are you surrounding yourself with? We evolve both through our own divine connection and energy source, and through who we spend time with and their level of consciousness. Many spiritual traditions encourage spending time with others on the path so that you can keep your energy high.

Freedom project: Put yourself in nourishing, nurturing and encouraging environments regularly.

77. Don't try to solve problems you don't have yet.

"If I had my life to live over, I would have a few more real problems and a lot less imaginary ones."
Nadine Stair at the age of 85

I once had a coaching conversation that went something like this, "I was about to start my enterprise but then got concerned that in two or three years time I might fall out of love with the work I am going to be doing, and then got worried about what I'd do if that happened. So I have decided not to start my business until I can figure out what I would do if that did happen." Duh! But that conversation really got me thinking about how resistance operates by trying to get us to waste precious time and energy by planning for and worrying about problems that we haven't got yet and probably won't ever have. It is a really pernicious but widespread form of resistance – trying to solve problems you don't yet have, and are likely to never have. In essence, worrying about the future and not acting now is resistance.

Freedom project: Spend the majority of your energy solving the problem and dealing with the issue that is right in front of you now: getting your first client, getting your blog up and running, writing your book. And what was my tip to the client? If you did fall out of love in three years time, you would have had three years of doing what you love, you'd have grown in confidence, talent and outlook, and you would find it easy to evolve into something else.

78. Get a few failures under your belt.

"Failure has benefits. I was set free by failure. My greatest fear had been realised and I was still alive. Rock bottom became a solid foundation on which I built my life. It taught me things I could never have learned about myself any other way."

JK Rowling, Author of Harry Potter series, at Harvard University Commencement speech.

I love the idea that if you don't want to make a mistake, but then you shouldn't get out of bed in the morning at all. Strange as it may sound, experiencing the pain of failure can be incredibly liberating. Failure is not something to avoid, it shows you are in the game playing rather than being a spectator. You plan, you prepare, you want guarantees, you do more research so you increase your chances of not getting it wrong. Failure won't kill you, and indeed can make you and help you find the strong foundations within you. Once you have failed and survived a few times, then you start to be liberated.

Freedom project: Just getting going with the quickest, easiest, lowest risk version of what you want to do so that you can succeed quickly and small and fail quickly and small. Why? So you can learn from both. So that you don't try to perfect something that is off track. Get it going and learn as you go, on the job. You can never get it right on the drawing board. Get it going and develop it live. Don't expect to get things right at the beginning. Why would you?

79. Don't resist the rehearsals, they lead you to mastery.

"Pursue mastery, not for the rewards it will bring you but for the person it will make you."

Robin Sharma, Author of
The Leader Who Had No Title

I loved watching a DVD of the making of *Love,* one of the six Cirque du Soleil shows permanently showing in Las Vegas. *Love* was a dream of collaboration for many years between Guy Labertiere, the creative director of Cirque, and George Harrison. When George died, they decided to bring the dream to fruition as a tribute to George. The programme documented the year of rehearsals for the show. Whilst individually they were all skilled athletes and performers, as an ensemble, they were, frankly, rubbish. They argued, they dropped each other, they wondered whether they'd ever get the moves right. They feared that Ringo Starr and Paul McCartney wouldn't like the show. The massive technology the show had in its purpose built theatre kept going wrong. But in time the performances improved, the team bonded and the technical problems were ironed out. When the show launched, it was great and received massive critical acclaim and is now regularly sold out. It takes practice to get good, usually a lot of practice. Much research now points to the reality that a level of mastery comes as result of at least 10,000 hours of practice of what you love. So don't resist the rehearsals, you are not supposed to be good when you begin! Learn, grow and eventually, master.

Freedom project: Practise, practise and practise. What do you need to invest time and love into getting good at? Do it!

80. Support your success by creating a supportive structure.

"The professional is on a mission. He will not tolerate disorder. He eliminates chaos from his world in order to banish it from his mind. He wants the carpet vacuumed and the threshold swept, so the Muse may enter and not soil her gown."

Steven Pressfield in *The War of Art*

Too much control in your life will kill your creativity, but too much chaos in your life will drain you of energy too. To be truly creatively free, you need life affirming structures in place. So structure your life to support your work – to succeed you need order and structure as well as creative freedom. A creatively successful life comes through a combination of creative freedom and structure that you fully support. What does structure look like? Stephen King reads every day and that inspires his writing. It's friendship and structuring time with those you love. It is quarantining energy drainers in your life. It is creating projects, goals and deadlines. It is getting coaching or mentoring support. It is surrounding yourself with loving and encouraging people. It is learning what you need to learn.

Freedom project: Identify three ways to support yourself through your resistance. Put those things in place.

81. Learn to self-validate.

"We are not valuable because we are a member of a certain group or because we call God by a certain name. We are not valuable because we follow a guru or observe a certain diet. We are valuable because we are a spark of the divine. And the only thing Gurus, priests, rabbis and elders can do for us is point us back in the direction of home, and home is, of course, within."

Darren John Main,
Yoga Teacher

Resistance thrives on your seeking approval. It wants you to give your sovereignty to others about what they think and feel about you and your work. Resistance wants you to let others define you and your capabilities. It has you believing that your value lies in pleasing others and gaining their approval. It has you believing that your worth is dependent on the reaction of others to you and your work. Your job isn't just to please, but to live fully, to be real and to contribute. Sometimes you serve best through challenging and causing a disturbance. Sometimes the people you serve will feel uncomfortable before they see the value in what you are offering. Your job is to receive inspired instructions and then craft and deliver those instructions and little by little be less concerned about their reception. To do this you will need to learn to self validate and self-love. That's not easy, as we have been conditioned for millennia to fear rejection and disapproval. Loss of approval, criticism or rejection can even feel like a threat to our psychic survival. The more you can be an unconditional friend to yourself, the more you can enjoy others but need their approval less.

Freedom project: Whose opinion are you giving too much power to? Whose definition of you are you struggling with? Affirm your own sovereignty – you are king or queen of your own inner kingdom.

82. Throw your heart over the fence and make a commitment.

"There is tremendous power in putting your ass where your heart wants to be."

Steven Pressfield,
Author of *The War of Art*

Commitment is the heartfelt choice to give yourself fully to something. We are all committed – the question is to what? We can be committed to being uncommitted, to sitting on the fence, to our stories and excuses or to suffering. We can be committed to showing up, to contribution, to love and healing our minds. So what are you most committed to? What do you want to be most committed to? Commitment is an ongoing process. I think as we grow up we can easily step back from life because of the wounds and fears we gather as we grow up, and we become less committed and less wholehearted. We hold back for fear of getting hurt again. I think by the time I was a teenager, I was only about 25% committed to life. I guess that today I am 50% committed and hope that increases as I mature even more. Holding back does not guarantee that you won't get hurt. As you give yourself to life, you will get hurt at times, misunderstood, even abused here and there. But most of the time you will have the pleasure of knowing that you are living fully.

Freedom project: What will you choose to make a commitment to today? What will you be wholehearted about?

Key 5:

Higher power and skilfulness – serving your brothers and sisters

Your resistance is your responsibility, but you are far from alone in summoning power to overcome it. Resistance and the hells it can create, resides within your ego, which is the principle of separation, and the consciousness of having been abandoned and left to our own devices. The support available to beat your resistance comes from your own resourcefulness, from earthly friends and allies, and also I believe, from a higher plane of consciousness, which through this book I have chosen to call Heaven. The universe is benevolent – it wants wonderful and beautiful things to happen and to exist. The universe doesn't just observe, it supports and assists. I do believe that there are forces of resistance within you and there are greater forces to help you overcome resistance which reside in that plane of consciousness. I always loved the quote by the mystic William Blake who said, "Eternity is in love with the creations of time." Unseen, at least with our eyes, forces of love, inspiration, encouragement and assistance are also available to us. Heaven is our ally in bringing our work and creations into existence in this realm. Dr Chuck Spezanno, one of my mentors, once said in a talk in London, "When we start our spiritual journey, it seems that there is a lot of us (our ego) and a little bit of Heaven. As we progress, there is less of us and more of

Heaven." That I believe is the whole journey we are on. We start off believing that we are alone and unassisted and gradually realise how loved and supported we are, but we were so caught up in our own dramas that we could not see it.

83. Inspiration is the doorway to the greater mind and resources.

"I don't have any of my own plans. I just wait for inspiration and then I know what I have to do."

Richard Barrett, Architect of Global Transformation and Author

You have a human mind and a divine mind. Resistance aims to distract you from your greater creative powers. When you are inspired you are uplifted and then the mortal human mind kicks back in and the resistance kicks in. When you are inspired, dormant forces, faculties and talents do come alive in you. You discover that you are greater than you thought you were.

Freedom project: Remember you are more than your human mind and logical thought and that you have access to other intelligences too.

84. Embrace the adventure into your creative being.

"Life is beautiful, we are powerful. We have a say in how our life unfolds and life is not something that happens to us, we happen to life. There are immutable truths even if you don't know them."

Mike Dooley,
Creator of *Notes from the Universe*

Did you have anyone who told you everyday growing up how powerful and creative you are? That you can consciously create a meaningful and exciting life for yourself? That you can happen to life rather than life seem to happen to you? Whether or not you did hear that message, it hasn't altered your nature as a creative being. Your power awaits your conscious embrace of it. It hasn't gone anywhere. You are naturally powerful and creative – that is your nature. You are a child of the great Creator and are able to create. The only question is: how are you using your creativity? In truth, most people use their creativity to deny their creativity. They create problems, obstacles, fears, excuses, rationalisations and stories about why they can't be truly creative, all the time unaware of how much creative energy it takes to block themselves. So what is the choice? To consciously use your creativity to build your life, to create new life, new ventures, new art, new joys. To bring into being things that didn't exist before, but do, because of you. We all have to invest in something – are you investing in fear and excuses or in love and creativity? Into excuses, or into creations and new life?

Freedom project: Enjoy discovering your potential and possibilities – discovering the amazing being that you are and exploring your inner universes.

85. Summon your visible assistance.

"I know of no greater joy than facilitating the happiness and well-being of another human being and giving people support to create what they want most in their lives."
Michael Neill, Success Coach

You are not alone, even if you feel it, and you needn't feel alone. Resistance is generated by your ego, and it aims to create a hell inside your consciousness. The ego tells you that resistance is actually trying to save you from hell, when actually it is the cause of some of your most hellish experiences. But you have assistance available to you. You can summon friends, mentors and collaborators. You can summon your inner resources of courage, love, inspiration, and determination. You can summon your own talent and gifts that may be lying dormant within you. We tend to celebrate the idea of independence and being self-made. That was always an illusion. There is the healthy independence of being responsible for yourself and your work, but the unhealthy side of independence is the belief that you can't or shouldn't ask for help, and if you get help then your success has been a cheat.

Freedom project: How can you increase the amount of support you both give and receive?

86. Summon your invisible assistance.

"As resistance works to keep us from being who we were born to be, equal and opposite powers are counter poised against it. These are our allies and angels."

Steven Pressfield, Author of *The War of Art*

You can also summon higher invisible forces of a more divine nature. Whether you think of them as Muses, the Universe, Love, God, Angels, Divine love, to me doesn't matter. What is important is that they do exist and they are supporting you. The ego is so attached to its independence and the reliance on its own power and will do all it can to resist you forming an active and more radical dependence and inter-dependence on these higher forces. There are forces that are unseen by our eyes that are both encouraging and actively supportive of us creating new life. They are planting inspired ideas in our minds so that we feel the impulse and desire to bring these creations into existence in this physical world. Love is a universal power which has its roots in the heart of creation, whilst fear and resistance only have the power within our own minds. Resistance is created through separation from our source. So here is my tip: Pray to align yourself with these higher forces and ask for their guidance and support in your ventures.

Freedom project: Spend time praying, contemplating and meditating on the treasures within you and the help that is available to you. Ask for help, believe you are worth loving and supporting. Receive help and give thanks in advance.

87. Recognise that the smarter you get, the smarter your resistance can become.

"The smarter and more accomplished I become, the smarter and more accomplished my resistance becomes."

Julia Cameron, after writing 32 books, musicals, screenplays and hundreds of articles

In February 2011, I had the pleasure of attending a two day Creativity Boot Camp in London with million-selling author of 32 books, Julia Cameron. I loved it and I knew I was in the presence of a true pro, someone who knew resistance well and still showed up to give her creative gifts to the world. I was blessed to film a short interview with her, and when I said to her half-jokingly, "One would imagine that after 32 books, many screenplays and musicals, you are beyond resistance", she looked me in the eye and shared the thought above. I was relieved rather than depressed to hear her say that. It validated my own experience. Resistance never goes away. Indeed, the more you access your own creative energy and gifts, the more and cunning ways resistance will generate to scare and distract you.

Freedom project: Grow in awareness of resistance and its strategies so you can continue to recognise and win over it. There is nothing wrong with you.

88. Invest in your life-long learning.

"In the new information society, where change is the only constant, we can no longer expect to get an education and be done with it. Like it or not, the information society has turned us all in to life long learners."

John Naisbit, Author of *Megatrends*

Whilst I have strongly suggested that the addiction to learning more before you start can be a form of resistance, I am also a passionate advocate of being a life-learner. There is so much to learn today, so invest in your own learning and personal growth. Learning is what most of us adults will do for at least part of our living in the 21st century. In 2005 I know I faced a challenge and needed to make a decision. My business partner, Niki Hignett, is nearly twenty years younger than me and grew up with the Internet and as a software engineer. He has grown up in a wired and connected world. Part of me was scared and didn't know how to engage with the digital world, but I knew if I didn't, then our success would be diminished. So I had to make a decision about whether I would learn more about the Internet and how the wired world worked. I am so glad I did as my personal fulfilment and business success leapt forward as a result. But it was a horrible experience to have to acknowledge my own ignorance and realise I couldn't just wing it, but needed to learn. Learning is now a lifelong activity, especially when you are an Inspired Entrepreneur, not just something we did at school and in formal education. So here is the tip: what *do* you really need to learn? Be honest and find a way of learning it soon.

Freedom project: Where are you ignorant? What are you inspired to learn? What do you want to learn? What do you need to learn? Go learn it from someone good.

89. Embrace life-long *un*learning.

"The first problem for all of us is not to learn but to unlearn."

Gloria Steinem, American Feminist, Journalist, and Social and Political Activist

Even though it is crucial to be able to learn, it is also vital to be able to unlearn. Knowing what to forget and what to let go of. Because the world is changing, what made you successful this year may sink you next year. Imagine being the producers of 78 records in the 1950's – you would have thought you had it made. Then came LP's (Long playing records) in the 1960's and the 78 was dead. Then came tapes and then CD's and pretty much killed LP's. And now MP3 downloads are killing the CD. All in 50 years – in one lifetime. Change is a constant and the rate of change is increasing. So being willing to let go of old ideas whilst at the same time holding onto eternal values like wisdom, kindness, love and collaboration is critical.

Freedom project: What have you learned or been taught that isn't serving you any more? Be willing to let it go and embrace something truer and more life-affirming.

90. Make friends with vulnerability and be willing to be broken open.

"The experience of change and transformation is never complete. Something bigger and brighter always calls to shine through us. We are continually challenged to change and grow, to break down and break through."
Elizabeth Lessor, Author of *Broken Open*

It is never the end of the line. Be willing to be vulnerable – be broken open. The ego is always trying to trick you into believing that it is the end of the line, time to die, to give up. But it's always an invitation into a greater life, a new chapter. A new beginning. Don't resist rock bottom. The only way is up. It can be cleansing. It can be liberating. It can be healing. Some people would rather die though than change their mind. Be willing to be wrong about how you've seen yourself so that you can discover who you truly are. Although there is nothing wrong with you, you may have to face all the beliefs that there is something wrong so that you can be released. We create defences around old wounds, and sometimes it's time to dismantle the defences, address our wounds and heal, so we no longer feel the pain. As you dismantle defences, you will have more energy and be more available.

Freedom project: Where do you need to allow yourself to become vulnerable, to not cope? What are you trying to hold together which may need to fall apart for a while and then be reformed? How can you get some support and understanding to do that?

91. Develop emotional maturity.

"It is human to have a long childhood; it is civilized to have an even longer childhood. Long childhood makes a technical and mental virtuoso out of man, but it also leaves a life-long residue of emotional immaturity in him."
Erik Homburger Erikson (1902-1994), Psychologist

Emotional maturity is the willingness and ability to learn to deal with bigger emotions and not to act them out or be overwhelmed by them. Often we bury our bigger and more painful emotions. We suppress them because we fear we could be overwhelmed by them. By developing the courage and capacity to feel bigger feelings, you will feel more alive, and comfortable within yourself. People are likely to feel more comfortable and safe around you too, so you become more attractive.

Freedom project: What have you been afraid of feeling? What could you have the courage to feel now and start freeing yourself from?

92. Value ease and shrink your areas of struggle.

"One of the saddest things in life is man's propensity to use force to get his way - to use the battering ram instead of the key to open doors."

Eric Butterworth, Author of *Spiritual Economics*

One form of resistance is an overlaying belief in struggle – everything has to be difficult and painful and involve sacrifice and pain. Not exactly inspiring, eh? Doesn't exactly make you want to take on anything, does it? We can be suspicious of anything that is not born of difficulty – our ego whispers, "That was too easy, it can't be useful or have any value." Learn to value and trust ease and grace – sometimes it can just be really easy. Resistance is of the ego and the ego thrives on struggle and difficulty. So when something is easy, we may resist it because we are suspicious. Sometimes you manage to receive inspiration, shape your idea, give it form and ship it before resistance really kicks in. We think we are deluded that anything could be so easy. Sometimes, rightly so. Sometimes things are too good to be true. But they need not be. There can be grace and ease and success without struggle. Reg Presley wrote the song *Love Is All Around* in about 10 minutes. He was inspired by the Joy Strings Salvation Army band he'd seen on TV, and the song has become a hit several times over and made him millions. It needn't be difficult. What is hard for our ego could be easy for our creative heart and spirit. I am not sure that spirit knows struggle, it just knows ease. It is always our ego that creates struggle and difficulty. There is a difference between investing energy and emotion in projects and struggling with them. Investment is a choice, struggle contains fear.

Freedom project: Let it be easy when you can. Where are you a little addicted to the struggle? Pray for ease. Choose ease. Value ease and grace.

93. Find your own value and significance.

"Leadership is communicating to people their worth and potential so clearly that they are inspired to see it in themselves. Are you such a leader?"

**Steven Covey,
Author and Teacher**

In *A Course in Miracles* it teaches us that "Heaven is incomplete without your joy." The Bible says, "You are the light of the world." Makes you feel kinda significant doesn't it? But you can't demand that people value you. It won't quite work to go up to people and say, "I am the light of the world, can you give me a little more respect please?" But you can learn to find that true value and significance within yourself. To know it about yourself and then extend it outwards. You can learn to truly love and value yourself or maybe more truthfully, you remember the value that you always had that you forgot. People treating us kindly remind us that we are worth being kind to. Being shown love and respect, remind us we are worth loving and respecting

Freedom project: How can you value and treasure yourself more truly? Where are you underestimating your significance?

94. Embrace meaninglessness.

"The ego offers meaning and even things to worship, such as idols of money, lust, romance or power, as if they would save us or make us happy. This eventually leads to greater disappointment or shattered dreams. Meaninglessness is the battleground between the ego and Heaven though Heaven doesn't fight. It simply offers the truth."

Dr Chuck Spezzano,
Spiritual Teacher and Author

One of the most horrible places of resistance is the place of meaninglessness. This is a place where at best we can't be bothered, and at worst, we want to keel over and die. You may have pursued some meaning – pleasing others, being loyal to a company or an institution and then been disappointed and wondered why you bothered. Meaninglessness is actually a birthing place where something of your true self wants to break through, but your ego is fighting your higher self and tries to distract you and tell you to keel over. The ego is always trying to create some new meaning to keep you occupied. The true meaning of life is love, to serve Love or Heaven. So if you get tempted by your ego into some new cul-de-sac, ask Heaven what meaning it would write upon your life. You are watched over by Heaven.

Freedom project: Ask yourself, "What is Heaven's meaning here?" Listen, trust and act on your answer.

95. Liberate yourself from attachment to outcomes so you can act freely.

"He who would be serene and pure needs but one thing: detachment."

Meister Eckhart, Mystic

One of the biggest forms of resistance is attachment – we won't act unless……. Think less about how your work is going to be received, whether it is going to get you adored and set the world on fire. Learn to start giving without conditions. You may resist acting when you feel very attached to the results of your action. When you can act from a place of being less attached to the outcome, you are actually more likely to get the outcome you want. My friend Kate built a successful executive coaching business by building a network of friends and advocates, but she did it by having conversations, making friends and offering to help. Paradoxically, the less she wanted from people, the more opportunities came her way. Do it because it's in your heart to do it. Do it for the love. Do it as a gift. Do it like you don't need anything in return and you'll receive so much in return. Have faith, trust and intelligence and act without attachment as much as possible. You have to have a lot of faith and trust. You just have to show up and offer what you have. And when you are truly following your Muse rather than trying to second guess the market, there will be an audience for your creations in this world.

Freedom project: Where do you need to act and share more without so much thought to results and outcomes?

96. As you share your gifts, the whole planet shifts.

"Every breath taken in by the man who loves, and the woman who loves, goes to fill the water tank, where the spirit horses drink."

Robert Bly, Poet

We are all part of one consciousness and your work is a drop in the ocean, and the ocean is made of drops. The physicists are telling us that on a quantum level we are all connected. On a conscious level, your work will touch people, but in the deeper collective mind, the groove that your happiness creates makes an impact. It contributes to lifting the energy of the whole consciousness. The whole world is blessed as you show up more fully and authentically. You make it a little easier for those who walk beside you and will come after you.

Freedom project: Show up for those you don't even know and for those still to come. Create a ripple. You have no idea of the impact of your love and brilliance.

97. Allow yourself to imagine the possibilities.

*"When asked if I am pessimistic or optimistic about the
future, my answer is always the same: If you look at
the science about what is happening on earth and aren't
pessimistic, you don't understand data. But if you meet the
people who are working to restore this earth and the lives of
the poor, and you aren't optimistic, you haven't got a pulse."*

**Paul Hawken, Environmentalist,
Entrepreneur, Journalist, and Author**

Within you there is a world waiting to be born. There is a
vision in your soul, a dream of the contribution that you
promised to make in transforming some corner of this world
and that will gladden your heart to do. In your heart you
remember the man or woman you promised to be and
know you will be. As St Catherine of Siena said, "Be who
God meant you to be and you will set the world on fire."
There is a part of you that is here to set the world on fire.
And there are endless possibilities within you. The spirit in
you knows no limits. You have within you all the instructions
you need to help midwife a new world. You are encoded
to play a wonderful role in helping to transform the world.
Your transformation of the world is in direct proportion to
the extent that you are willing to be transformed. What were
major problems for you, can become cornerstones and gifts
to share. As you transform your own hells, you inspire others
to their capacity to transform theirs. Your ego will put limits
on and dismiss your grand visions, because it can never see,
how you are going to do it.

Freedom project: Shift your focus and keep asking
yourself the question, "How good could this get? What
are the great possibilities here? What are the seeds that
are waiting to grow and blossom in you?"

98. Without a belief in a higher power, you could well be screwed!

"Spiritual power is omnipresent. It is released…by spiritualizing our consciousness. This divine energy will surge through us as we erase negative thoughts from consciousness and become one with God-mind."

**Charles Fillmore, Author and Father
of the Unity Church Movement**

The ego does not really change itself willingly. It may change itself on the surface level, but its underlying dynamics of fear and separation remain. As Einstein says, most problems can't be solved at the level of understanding at which they were created. The ego actually loves the problems it creates, as it is afforded power and control through them. True and deep transformation only happens through the surrendering of the ego. By surrendering a corner of our life to start with, or the whole of our life if we are feeling really brave, to a greater intelligence, we evolve our consciousness. Our great need is for evolution in our awareness and understanding. Most people have trouble believing today that there is a greater intelligence. There is a great trend for disproving God. And even if we believe in God, we find it hard to believe that God is remotely interested in us and our life, so we keep our hand on the steering wheel, believing that by letting go of the steering wheel, we will crash into the trees.

Freedom project: What do you need to surrender? What needs to be done through you?

99. Resistance is an invitation to integrate your inner masculine and inner feminine.

"Inside every person are the energies of the divine masculine and the divine feminine. This has nothing to do with being a man or a woman."

Art Giser, Founder of Energetic NLP

The inner masculine and feminine are not about gender but are more about universal energies that you can embody. The feminine is about receptivity, allowing ideas and concepts to enter your consciousness through inspiration and intuition and then creating a safe space within you to tend them. The feminine is obviously about nurturing and encouraging ideas to flourish and grow. Resistance operates here when you are too quick to dismiss ideas that seem too big, exciting and beautiful. You don't allow things to flourish within you. The masculine is about taking action, creating an impact and causing things to happen and having an effect. Resistance operates here when you know what you need and want to be doing, when ideas have bubbled away inside and grown inside you, but you simply don't act.

Freedom project: There is a time for gestation and incubation and inner growth and there is a time for taking action and putting things out into the world. Don't get over-pregnant. Where you do need to create more of a nurturing space within yourself for things to grow and develop? Where do you need to take more direct action? Do you need to do more of both?

100. Resistance can come out of nowhere and temporarily blindside you.

"We were doing so great. Our project was in high gear. We were almost finished, then everything crashes. The big crash is so predictable across almost all fields of enterprise that we can almost set our watch by it."
Steven Pressfield in *Do The Work*.

Suddenly everything can be going well and you think you have beaten your resistance, you think you've accessed the slipstream and become a functional and creative being. Then wham! You get temporarily side-swiped, usually just on the cusp of a new level of success. You leave the track. You crash and burn and you didn't even see it coming. Some big whale of a piece of resistance suddenly rises out of the deep of your subconscious mind and overturns you. Let me give you a quick example. In December 2009 I started writing my sixth book and then resistance got me and I gave up on it. I started again in May 2010 and got through my resistance, got it completed and edited and published. Two days before the book launch on December 16th 2010, I went to pick the books up from the printer and nearly wept with joy at how good I felt and how great the book looked. I had a few hours of tremendous pride. Then these thoughts started creeping into mind: "But only my editor and the publisher have read the book – maybe they didn't really like it and they just didn't have the heart to tell me. Maybe I have actually written a crap book and tomorrow night over 100 people are going to get copies and I am going to look so stupid and alienate people. Maybe I should cancel the launch event, burn all the books and pretend I never wrote it!" Mad as that sounds, it's what my resistance was telling me. I actually found it quite hard to enjoy the actual launch event, but I pushed through and 120 people came. I have subsequently had tremendous feedback for the book. But I was shocked, how even at the last hurdle, my resistance kicked in and tried to get me to sabotage my efforts.

Freedom project: Be kind to yourself when a new and unexpected slice of resistance emerges – it shows you are growing and showing up more fully.

101. Your true creative expression is a gift to the world.

"When you step beyond a fear or challenge, you help many more people than yourself."

Alan Cohen, Author and Teacher

Your ego will try to convince you that your desire to show up with your gifts is nothing more than selfish attention seeking behaviour. But true creative expression is both a gift and a blessing to us all. I remember a conversation with my friend, Richard Olivier, founder of the Olivier Mythodrama project. Growing up as the child of two creative and successful actors, Sir Lawrence Olivier and Joan Plowright, he knew a thing or two about fame and creativity. He told me, "You can use fame and attention to meet your own needs and to try to feel good about yourself, or you can use fame and visibility to bless, inspire and encourage." Use your creative gifts to serve us all. You help nudge us all a little closer to Heaven. So please, give us what you've got, we need it.

Freedom project: Honour the generous spirit in your heart that wants to contribute to the lives of your brothers and sisters and life on this planet.

Conclusion:

In 2009, I was co-presenting a three-day workshop at the University of Cape Town, in South Africa in their School of Executive Development. My colleague, Shadrick Muzzaza, said to the group, "Liberating myself from the tyranny of my own mind is far greater than the challenge of liberating this country from apartheid." Something about Shadrick's comment touched me deeply. We can over throw tyrants and governments and laws, but the greatest liberation of all is freeing ourselves from the tyranny of *our mind and thinking* so we can liberate our own self-in-potential, the reason we are on this planet. Truly, the greatest triumphs of all are the triumphs of our "higher self" over our "lower self." I wish you every success in your own journey of liberation, so that you can let your own light shine and your own brilliance out.

Far more often you find your dreams of art shattered by your resistance. You give in to the fear and your art ends up lying in a box somewhere unseen. Please don't let this be you. There are so many allies and friends cheering you on to succeed and bring your love and gifts into this world. So much wants to come into this world through you. So please, put your heart in Heaven's hands and allow yourself to be inspired. Turn up the volume on your inner spirit and genius and recognise and win over your resistance. We need your love, gifts and passion in the world. Please give us what you've got. On the other side of your resistance new chapters of love, creativity, success, happiness and abundance are beckoning to you.

Please show up with the love God gave you – we need you. As it reminds us in *A Course in Miracles* "The light in you is what the universe longs to behold." Give us your love and your light.

I am cheering you on!

Join the Inspired Entrepreneur Community now for £1!

Nick Williams and his business partner, Niki Hignett, love helping you reach your potential and have created the Inspired Entrepreneur Community in London, and globally too, to support you. Membership includes between one and three talks a month, gatherings, workshops, retreats and teleseminars. It will give you the inspiration, knowledge, know-how and the sense of community you need to support you and your entrepreneurial dreams.

- Premium membership costs just £12.99 per month and you can try the first month for just £1.

- Silver membership is just £4.99 a month and is for you if you can't attend the live events, enabling you access to all the downloads. Again, you can try the first month for just £1.

So if you'd like to invite Nick to speak to your group, retain him to coach or mentor you, or join the Inspired Entrepreneur Community, please contact him by any of the means below:

Nick Williams
nick@inspired-entrepreneur.com
www.inspired-entrepreneur.com
Daily Inspiration on Twitter: @nickwilliams1

Blog: www.inspired-entrepreneur.com/blog
Facebook: www.inspired-entrepreneur.com/facebook/nick
Tel. 020 8 346 1551

Nick Williams,
Heart at Work,
PO Box 2236,
London, W1A 5UA

Nick Williams is passionate about helping people discover the work they were born to do and build successful businesses around that work. He'd love to help you.

His main services are:

- Keynote speaking

- Workshops

- Coaching and mentoring

- Broadcasting

Please contact his office direct if you would like to get Nick involved in your project.

Other books by Nick Williams

The Work We Were Born To Do

The 12 Principles of The Work We Were Born To Do

Unconditional Success

Powerful Beyond Measure

How to Be Inspired

The Business You Were Born To Create